Single-Session Coaching and One-At-A-Time Coaching

In *Single-Session Coaching and One-At-A-Time Coaching: Distinctive Features*, Windy Dryden presents a clear and accessible overview of the theory and practice of Single-Session Coaching and One-At-A-Time Coaching (SSC/OAATC). Presented in the highly accessible Distinctive Features format, Dryden explores how these approaches allow coaches and clients to tackle problems and find solutions quickly and flexibly.

Single-Session Coaching and One-At-A-Time Coaching is split in two parts, providing a complete understanding of both the theory and practice of SSC/OAATC, as well as clearly examining key topics, including the foundations of SSC/OAATC, what makes a good SSC/OAATC coach and coachee, common misconceptions, preparing for and structuring a session, and considering significant coachee variables. It explains key terminology, such as the difference between Problem-Focused and Development-Focused SSC/OAATC, and portrays these differences in useful case studies to show the benefits of each for individual clients. Finally, it concludes with details on following up with the coachee, including key questions to ask.

With case studies throughout, this approach can be applied in various clinical settings, such as primary care, and non-clinical settings, such as voluntary sectors, and is ideal for time-limited scenarios in comparison to other, more time-consuming, coaching methods. This will be an invaluable tool for coaches in practice and in training, as well as for academics and students of coaching.

Windy Dryden, PhD., is in clinical and consultative practice and is an international authority on Cognitive Behaviour Therapy. He is Emeritus Professor of Psychotherapeutic Studies at Goldsmiths, University of London. He has worked in psychotherapy for more than 40 years and is the author or editor of over 230 books.

Coaching Distinctive Features
Series Editor: Windy Dryden

Leading practitioners and theorists of coaching approaches write simply and briefly on what constitutes the main features of their particular approach. Each book highlights thirty main features, divided between theoretical and practical points. Written in a straightforward and accessible style, they can be understood by both those steeped in the coaching tradition and by those outside that tradition. The series editor is Windy Dryden.

Titles in the series:

Rational Emotive Behavioural Coaching
Windy Dryden

Cognitive Behavioural Coaching
Michael Neenan

Acceptance and Commitment Coaching
Jon Hill and Joe Oliver

Psychodynamic Coaching
Claudia Nagel

Single-Session Coaching and One-At-A-Time Coaching
Windy Dryden

For further information about this series, please visit
www.routledge.com/Coaching-Distinctive-Features/book-series/CDF

Single-Session Coaching and One-At-A-Time Coaching

Distinctive Features

Windy Dryden

LONDON AND NEW YORK

First published 2020
by Routledge
2 Park Square, Milton Park, Abingdon, Oxon OX14 4RN

and by Routledge
52 Vanderbilt Avenue, New York, NY 10017

Routledge is an imprint of the Taylor & Francis Group, an informa business

© 2020 Windy Dryden

The right of Windy Dryden to be identified as author of this work has been asserted by him in accordance with sections 77 and 78 of the Copyright, Designs and Patents Act 1988.

All rights reserved. No part of this book may be reprinted or reproduced or utilised in any form or by any electronic, mechanical, or other means, now known or hereafter invented, including photocopying and recording, or in any information storage or retrieval system, without permission in writing from the publishers.

Trademark notice: Product or corporate names may be trademarks or registered trademarks, and are used only for identification and explanation without intent to infringe.

British Library Cataloguing-in-Publication Data
A catalogue record for this book is available from the British Library

Library of Congress Cataloging-in-Publication Data
A catalog record has been requested for this book

ISBN: 978-0-367-34773-4 (hbk)
ISBN: 978-0-367-34775-8 (pbk)
ISBN: 978-0-429-32787-2 (ebk)

Typeset in Times New Roman
by Newgen Publishing UK

Contents

Preface	vii

Part I THEORY — 1

1	Introducing Single-Session Coaching and One-At-A-Time Coaching (SSC/OAATC)	3
2	What is Single-Session Coaching (SSC) and One-At-A-Time Coaching (OAATC)?	7
3	The foundations of SSC/OAATC	11
4	People can be helped in one session of coaching or in one coaching session at a time	17
5	The single session and one-at-a-time mindset and mode of delivery	21
6	Why SSC/OAATC?	23
7	Development-focused SSC/OAATC	29
8	Problem-focused SSC/OAATC	33
9	The working alliance in SSC/OAATC	37
10	What makes a good SSC/OAATC coach and coachee?	41
11	Misconceptions of SSC/OAATC	45

Part II PRACTICE — 49

12	Good practice in SSC/OAATC	51
13	What not to do in SSC/OAATC	57
14	Placing SSC/OAATC in context	59
15	Responding to the first contact	63
16	Contracting for SSC/OAATC	67
17	Structuring the session effectively	71
18	Preparing for the session: The pre-session telephone conversation	77
19	Beginning the session	85

20 Creating and keeping to a meaningful focus in the session	89
21 Agreeing on a development-based process objective or problem-based process goal	93
22 Identifying and utilising important coaching variables in the session	99
23 Facilitating change in SSC/OAATC: General factors	105
24 Facilitating change in development-focused SSC/OAATC	113
25 Facilitating change in problem-focused SSC/OAATC	117
26 Action planning and implementation in development-focused SSC/OAATC	123
27 Rehearsing, action planning and implementing the solution in problem-focused SSC/OAATC	125
28 Identifying and dealing with roadblocks	131
29 Summarising, moving forward and tying-up loose ends	135
30 Following-up	139
Notes	143
References	147
Index	151

Preface

This book carries on the tradition of single-session and one-at-a-time interventions in the helping professions that was first crystallised by publications in the 1980s and 1990s by Bernard Bloom (1981, 1992) and Moshe Talmon (1990) – see Chapter 1. At the time, this work provided a wake-up call even for those who could see the value of brief therapy but had not thought that much could be achieved in a single session. As this book shows, it can! While Single-Session Coaching is currently being practised, as several websites of coaches in Britain and North America attest (see Chapter 8), this is the first book-length publication, as far as I am aware, on what I call 'Single-Session Coaching and One-At-A-Time Coaching' (SSC/OAATC) and as such it breaks new ground.

My thinking on single-session and one-at-a-time interventions has been shaped by Moshe Talmon, Michael Hoyt and Jeff Young, all of whom have been generous in giving their time by responding to my requests for information and for their views. I also wish to thank Jenny Forge who is using Single-Session Coaching to help psychiatrists in Britain further their professional development. Jenny's often stimulating questions have also helped to shape my thinking in this area. While all these people have been helpful, only I should be held responsible for what appears in this book. I hope to share my passion for this work here and hope that it stimulates your interest in this new development in the field of coaching.

Windy Dryden
March, 2019
London and Eastbourne

Part I

THEORY

Introducing Single-Session Coaching and One-At-A-Time Coaching (SSC/OAATC)

Why a book on Single-Session Coaching and One-At-A-Time Coaching[1]? Simply because some people seek out single sessions of coaching or only want such sessions scheduled one at a time rather than contract for a 'block' of coaching sessions. Also, as a quick internet search will reveal, a number of coaches offer Single-Session Coaching (see Chapter 14). As such, in this book, I present 30 distinctive features of SSC/OAATC focusing on both its theoretical and practical distinctive features as prescribed in the series in which the book appears – 'Coaching Distinctive Features' series.

Single-Session Coaching (SSC)/One-At-A-Time Coaching (OAATC) vs Single-Session Therapy (SST)/One-At-A-Time Therapy (OAATT)

SSC/OAATC is derived from SST/OAATT but tends to have a different focus. I use the word 'tends' here advisedly as will soon become clear. Thus SST/OAATT largely deals with what is going wrong in a person's life from a psychological perspective. The goal of SST/OAATT is to help that person to find a solution to their problem or begin this process so that they may get on with their life. In SSC/OAATC the person is relatively problem free but has a sense that they could get more out of themself, their job, their relationships or their life in general. The goal of SSC/OAATC is to help them to take the first steps to move towards such development.

Disturbance – dissatisfaction – development

The therapy/coaching approach with which I have been associated for many years – Rational Emotive Behaviour Therapy and Coaching – makes a useful distinction among three foci in therapy and coaching: i) disturbance; ii) dissatisfaction and iii) development (Dryden, 2015).

When taking a *disturbance* focus, the practitioner helps the person deal with their unhealthy, disturbed reactions to adversity. This is usually the domain of the therapist rather than the coach.

When taking a *dissatisfaction* focus, the practitioner helps the person deal with their feelings of dissatisfaction with the adversity. In this case, the person does not have (or no longer has) disturbed feelings about the adversity. If the person has had disturbed feelings and has been helped with these and is now addressing their feelings of dissatisfaction, then this is usually the domain of the therapist. When the person, from the start, only has feelings of dissatisfaction then this is usually the domain of the coach. While adopting a dissatisfaction focus, the therapist or coach helps the person to take steps to change the adversity if it can be changed or to adjust constructively if it can't be changed and then move on.

When taking a *development* focus, the practitioner helps the person deal with the situation where they are not facing an adversity about which they have disturbed or dissatisfied feelings, but where they are doing OK in life, but have a sense that they could get more out of that life in certain respects. This is usually the domain of the coach.

So far, the discussion concerning the differences between coaching and therapy has assumed that definite and clear distinctions can be made based on the foci adopted by both. However, in practice, this is not always the case, and I will discuss two situations in which the lines of demarcation between therapy and coaching are blurred.

People experience problems in coaching

It sometimes happens in coaching that when a coachee[2] is working towards a coaching objective[3] that they experience an adversity to which they respond in a disturbed manner. In this sense, the coach, if they have the skills to do so, helps the person deal with their problem before returning to their development-focused work. Thus, sometimes the coach has to do the work of the therapist in coaching, but they should do so only if they have the requisite skills as noted earlier.

People with problems sometimes come for coaching, not therapy

In an ideal world, people who have an emotional problem would seek help from a therapist while someone who does not have such a problem at the outset and wants help to use more of their potential in life would seek help from a coach. However, this is not an ideal world, and increasingly people are turning to coaches for help with their emotional problems. While it is not clear why this might be the case, my guess is that it is more acceptable for some people to consult a coach for their problems than a therapist. It is less self-stigmatising to do so.

Single-Session Coaching (SSC)/One-At-A-Time Coaching (OAATC) has its origins in Single-Session Therapy (SST)/One-At-A-Time Therapy (OAATT)

As I mentioned earlier, SSC/OAATC is derived from SST/OAATT. While the origins of the latter can be traced back to Freud (see Freud & Breuer, 1895 and Kuehn, 1965), modern-day SST/OAATT can be traced to the writings of Bernard Bloom (1981, 1992) who initiated and developed an approach that he termed, 'focused single-session therapy', and Moshe Talmon (1990, 1993) who together with Michael Hoyt and Richard Rosenbaum carried out pioneering work on SST at the Kaiser Permanente Clinic in San Francisco, California. Talmon had moved from doing ongoing therapeutic work in a private practice in Israel to the Kaiser Permanente which was a public clinic. Shocked and intrigued by the fact that a number of his clients only attended for one session, he decided to find out why and made 200 telephone calls to these clients whom most of his colleagues regarded as 'drop-outs' from treatment. What Talmon learned from these clients made him rethink many of the assumptions he held about therapy.

He found that of these 200 clients 78% reported that they had received what they wanted from therapy and only 10% said that they did not like the therapist or the outcome of therapy. Following on from that retrospective analysis, Hoyt, Talmon and Rosenbaum (1990) conducted a prospective study on planned Single-Session Therapy with 60 clients, 58 of whom were reached on follow-up. Of the 58, there were 34 that did not require further therapy, 88% reported "much improvement" or "improvement" and 79% thought that SST was sufficient for them.

From those early days, SST has grown in popularity and is now a service delivery model that is offered by appointment or by walk-in across the world. It is particularly popular in Australia and Canada where the first two international symposia for single-session and walk-in services were held respectively (Hoyt & Talmon, 2014; Hoyt, Bobele, Slive, Young & Talmon, 2018). As the field grew, Bloom's (1981, 1992) and Talmon's (1990, 1993) early work on SST has been developed in a number of different ways. For example, 'One-At-A-Time' Therapy (OAATT) occurs when a person has a session of therapy and may have more sessions, but can only book them one at a time. Blocks of sessions cannot be booked (Hoyt, 2011).

Single-Session Coaching (SSC) and One-At-A-Time Coaching (OAATC) is another recent development from SST/OAATT and is the focus of the current book.

What is Single-Session Coaching (SSC) and One-At-A-Time Coaching (OAATC)?

In this chapter, I will consider the nature of Single-Session Coaching (SSC) and One-At-A-Time Coaching (OAATC).

The nature of Single-Session Coaching (SSC)

SSC means one session

When most people hear about SSC, perhaps understandably they think that this refers to one session of coaching and that is all. And indeed, there are situations, for whatever reason, a person only has one coaching session. Here are a number of such scenarios:

Scenario 1. Michael wants to develop himself at work and seeks to do this primarily by himself, but wants to have a single coaching session to talk a few issues over with a coach and to develop a logical action plan. He and his coach contract for one session.

Scenario 2. Bettany is in training to be a coach and has been exposed to a number of different approaches to coaching during her training. She is being trained in the GROW model (Whitmore, 2017), but has read about Rational Emotive Behavioural Coaching (REBC) and wants to experience this approach in action as a coachee. She discovers that I practise this approach (Dryden, 2018a), contacts me, explains what she is looking for and we contract for a single session of REBC.

Scenario 3. Adriana volunteered for a demonstration of coaching with me when I was giving a coaching workshop in Brazil. She was being coached but was currently experiencing an obstacle towards her development-based objective and volunteered for the demonstration session for help with this obstacle. She knew that we were going to have one session and that it was unlikely we would ever meet again.

These three scenarios cover a variety of contexts for SSC. The first points to the coach's wish to take charge of the coaching process for himself in a single session with a coach to get him started. The second outlines the educational value for a coach in training to learn experientially about a different coaching approach while the third has a dual purpose. The workshop volunteer wishes to gain help for herself to address a coaching obstacle but is also prepared to discuss the issue in front of a group of her peers to facilitate their learning about SSC.

Scenario 4. A large national auditing company has decided to run a pilot scheme for a group of staff to help them pursue developmental objectives. They decide to launch a Single-Session Coaching service for volunteers and bring in three coaches experienced in brief coaching to staff the service.

This latter scenario describes a situation where an organisation with limited resources wishes to do something to help its employees to develop themselves and is prepared to pilot a scheme based on brief coaching, in this case SSC.

A single session of coaching, but more is available

In the current field of Single-Session Therapy (SST) it is generally agreed that the term 'Single-Session Therapy' describes the following situation. A therapist and a client agree to meet with the agreed intention to help the client find a solution to a problem and utilise strengths and skills to implement this solution in the understanding that further help is available if needed.

Extrapolating from this, we may say that Single-Session Coaching describes the following situation. A coach and a coachee agree to meet with the expressed intention to help the coachee find a way to enhance their development or to address an obstacle to a development-based objective on the understanding that further coaching is available if needed.

The nature of One-At-A-Time Coaching (OAATC)

OAATC can be seen as Single-Session Coaching in that the intention is to help the coachee get what they are looking for from the session so that they can get on with the business of developing themself in a nominated area of their life on their own, secure that they can return in the future to have another session if they need to. As Michael Hoyt (personal communication, 4/5/18) recently stated, "one-at-a-time doesn't necessarily mean only one time". However, before booking another session, the coachee is encouraged to commit to a period of reflection, digestion, action and letting time pass (Dryden, 2019a) – see Chapter 29.

Here are the main features of OAATC:

- The coachee has a session of coaching.
- The coachee is encouraged to take time after this session to a) reflect on and digest what they have learned from the session, b) take appropriate action based on this digested learning, c) experiment with other ways of furthering their development and d) let time pass and allow things to settle down.
- At the end of this period, the coachee decides whether or not to book another session of coaching.
- If they have another session, the same process is followed as earlier.
- The person can only book one session at a time. They cannot book a series of coaching sessions.

The OAATC framework allows the coachee to focus on their development one session at a time, to come and go as they please and to have another session whenever they feel that they can benefit from it.

The foundations of SSC/OAATC

In this chapter, I will present a number of ideas that underpin the practice of Single-Session Coaching and One-At-A-Time Coaching (SSC/OAATC).

Even a brief encounter can be helpful

Two decades ago. I was travelling by plane to a conference in the US and was seated next to a man who spent a lot of the journey meditating, as it turned out. Halfway into the flight, he opened his eyes and asked me about the purpose of my visit. We struck up a conversation about helping people and being helped, and he told me about something his grandfather told him which had influenced him as he faced uncertainty about what to do in life. His grandfather said to him, "My boy uncertainty is like fog. From afar it is thick, but if you walk into it, your vision clears a bit". The man let out a sigh followed by a little laugh, closed his eyes and went back to his meditation. I have remembered this piece of advice ever since, and whenever I am faced with uncertainty and am tempted to stop in my tracks, I move forward a little in the direction I was heading, and things do get a little clearer. Have I remembered this piece of advice because of its inherent good sense, the eccentricity of the man who told me the story or a combination of both? It is difficult to tell. Indeed, this is not the point. The point is that I was helped to deal with uncertainty through a very brief encounter. If humans could not be thus influenced, Single-Session Coaching would probably not exist.

The length of a coaching contract is expandable and influences the work done

Imagine that you are contacted by a woman who seeks coaching and is being sponsored by the organisation in which she works for ten coaching sessions. Over the phone, she gives you an idea of what she wants to achieve, and you agree to offer her a ten-session coaching contract. Three days before her first appointment she contacts you again and tells you that due to unexpected cuts suffered by the organisation that her boss can only agree to fund a single coaching session and she does not have the money to cover the rest of the cost. She is still very keen to see you for a single session and urges you to see her. What do you do? If you decide to offer her a Single-Session Coaching contract doing so will probably influence the work that you will do with her. You could both 'grasp the nettle' and work together to determine just how much you could achieve in that one session. If you make this decision, you are halfway to becoming a single-session coach. If you consider the differences between what you would do in that one session and what you would do over the course of ten sessions, then you will begin to see some of the central ingredients of Single-Session Coaching.

Much can be achieved from SSC/OAATC if certain ingredients are present

It is useful to consider SSC/OAATC as a plant. Certain ingredients will help it to flourish, and others will lead it to wither. In this section, I will outline three ingredients which, if present, will lead the coachee to get the most from SSC/OAATC.

The coach and coachee need to embark intentionally on SSC/OAATC

SSC/OAATC is not a way of working that can be imposed on a coachee, nor is it a way that can be suddenly introduced to them.

Instead, in order for the coachee to get the most from SSC/OAATC both the coach and coachee need to embark on this process with intention. This means that the coach needs to inform the coachee about the nature of SSC/OAATC so that the latter gives their informed consent to proceed.

The coach and coachee share realistic expectations about what can be achieved from SSC/OAATC

If the coachee has unrealistically high or unrealistically low expectations from SSC/OAATC then they will be disappointed in the first case and will not gain much at all from the process in the second case. So, what can be realistically expected from SSC/OAATC? In my view, the answer to this question depends on what type of coaching we are talking about. In development-focused coaching where the emphasis is on helping the coachee to develop themself, the goal of SSC/OAATC is to encourage the coachee to set a development-based objective, plan a pathway towards this objective and commit to launching this plan. In problem-focused coaching,[1] the goal is to help the coachee to solve the problem. Sometimes the person may have solved their problem at the end of the session. Most of the time it is not expected that the problem will be solved at the end of the session although if it is, so much the better. What is more likely is that the person is able to get unstuck and work towards problem resolution after the session has ended.

The coachee is ready to work, and the coach capitalises on that readiness

If one takes the variables 'ready to coach' and 'ready to be coached', then it is only when the coachee is ready to be coached and the coach is ready to coach that the power of SSC/OAATC can be fully realised.

Coachees can use internal and external resources to help themselves in SSC/OAATC

As discussed in the Chapter 1, the focus of coaching is on development – helping the coachee to get the most out of themself. In order for the coach to encourage the coachee to get the most from SSC/OAATC then they will need to help the person to use their internal strengths and resiliency factors. There is no time in SSC/OAATC to help the coachee to develop new strengths, so the emphasis needs to be on encouraging the person to use the best of what they already have in their repertoire.

Similarly, the potential of SSC/OAATC can be best harnessed when the coachee can be shown that they can use relevant resources in the environment in the pursuit of their development-based objective.

The coach structures the session effectively

The coach who structures the single session effectively will increase the chances that the coachee will get the most out of SSC/OAATC. Hoyt (2000, 2018) has outlined one such structure. He argues that after a pre-session conversation, the purpose of which is to help the coachee prepare for the session so that they get the most out of it, the session has four phases.

The early phase

Here, the coach draws upon the pre-session conversation, if they have had one with the coachee, builds the coaching alliance (see Chapter 9) and negotiates a development-based objective or a problem-based goal with the coachee.

The middle phase

Here, in development-focused coaching, the work is centred on helping the coachee to plan to take action to pursue their objectives and in problem-focused coaching change-based refocusing is facilitated, and solutions for change are discussed, selected and rehearsed.

The late phase

Here, in development-focused coaching, potential obstacles are identified and addressed, and in problem-focused coaching, action planning is done. Then in both forms of coaching leave-taking takes place. This termination phase is where the possibility for future sessions is discussed and a follow-up planned.

The follow-up phase

At follow-up, if it occurs, evaluation takes place, and coachee feedback is given. More help is available if needed.

ONE SESSION OF COACHING/ONE COACHING SESSION

People can be helped in one session of coaching or in one coaching session at a time

The traditional approach to coaching is that the coach and coachee contract for the former to help the latter to set and work towards meeting development-based objectives. The assumption here is that coach and coachee will meet regularly over time until a number of conditions have been met:

1. The coachee has met their objectives and has a plan in place to maintain and even enhance their coaching gains.
2. The coachee is making good progress towards meeting their objectives and opts to continue the remaining work on their own.
3. The coachee has identified and overcome an obstacle to meeting an objective and wishes to carry on their coaching work on their own.

This traditional approach to the work of coaching is not in question here, and I am not suggesting that SSC/OAATC should replace ongoing coaching. What I am suggesting is that there are times when the coach and coachee may choose a) to meet for a single session of coaching with the expressed aim of using that session for a particular purpose and with the agreed understanding that more coaching will be available if needed or b) to set up a contract where coaching will be available one session at a time and that while the coachee may only require one session, it is again understood that more sessions are available if needed.

In each case, it is clear to both parties from the outset that ongoing sessions are not a part of the coaching contract, but that the contract may be renegotiated so that ongoing work is the newly contracted service.

The question that I want to consider in this chapter is whether a person can derive benefit from their engagement with SSC/OAATC. My answer is in the affirmative.

What can be achieved in a single session?

If you recall, in this book, I will address two types of coaching[1]:

- Development-focused coaching where the focus is on coachee development and
- Problem-focused coaching where the focus is on a problem that the person wants to address. This problem may be a commonplace emotional problem (one of mild or moderate severity that lies within the coach's level of expertise to address) that is experienced either a) as a result of the person taking steps in coaching to achieve their development-based goal (referred to in this book as an obstacle) or b) in the course of their life and unrelated to coaching.

What can be achieved in a single session of development-focused coaching

In brief development-focused coaching (see Dryden, 2017a), the coach and coachee have a number of tasks to implement:

- To identify a *domain* of the coachee's life that will frame the work. Such domains may include work, family, recreational, relational or health to name but a few and can, of course, impact on one another.
- To set a *development-based objective* within the selected life domain that will become the focus of the work. If this objective is based on a significant value held by the coachee and if it can be integrated into their life, these factors will increase the chances that the coachee will pursue the objective when the going gets tough.

- To set a *signpost* towards the achievement of the development-based objective. This serves as a point, if reached, where the coachee is likely to be confident that they are well on the way to achieving their objective.
- To develop an action plan which will frame the coachee's pursuit of the signpost in the first case and of the objective in the second case. It is important that this plan can be integrated into the person's life as much as possible.
- To anticipate and plan to deal with potential obstacles to the implementation of the action plan.

The critical question here is how much of this can be achieved in a single session of coaching. If both coach and coachee set out with the intention of doing this work in one session and there are no complications and/or complexities, then much, if not all, of this work can be done in a single session. While I personally keep to the 50-minute coaching hour in my practice of SSC, other coaches who work very briefly with coachees offer extended sessions to cover all the ground outlined earlier. I have seen anything from 90 minutes to three hours mentioned concerning the length of an SSC session.

If more coaching time is needed, then don't forget that such time can be offered under the SSC umbrella. As I stated in Chapter 2:

Single-Session Coaching describes the following situation. A coach and a coachee agree to meet with the expressed intention to help the coachee find a way to enhance their development or to address an obstacle to a development-based objective in the understanding that further coaching is available if needed.

What can be achieved in a single session of problem-focused coaching?

In brief problem-focused coaching (see Dryden, 2017a), the coach and coachee have a number of tasks to implement:

- To identify the problem
- To set a problem-based goal

- To address the problem and find a potential solution
- To develop an action plan which will frame the pursuit of the problem-related goal
- To anticipate and plan to deal with potential obstacles to the implementation of the action plan

Again, the question is how much of this work can be achieved within a single session.

I have been doing problem-focused coaching for many years, mainly within the context of live demonstrations of single-session work in front of a professional work audience and I know that, again, if both coach and coachee set out with the intention of solving the problem then much can be achieved in the single session (Dryden, 2018b, 2019b). Thus, the coachee can be helped to get unstuck with respect to the problem and move on with their life, or they can be helped to address the obstacle to developmental-focused coaching effectively and to resume such work.

What can be achieved in one session at a time?

In One-At-A-Time Coaching, the coach and coachee contract to have coaching sessions that occur one at a time rather than in a time-limited block or ongoing. In one sense SSC and OAATC are indistinguishable. This is when the coach and coachee intend to achieve the tasks outlined earlier in one session but will use more if necessary. Where they are different is where the coach and coachee in OAATC agree to meet for one session at a time without the expectation that the work will be done in one session.

In the latter situation, the coach and coachee work to achieve one or two of the tasks outlined earlier. Then the coachee will engage in a period of reflection-digestion-action-letting time pass and will then have another coaching session to engage in another set of tasks. The work proceeds in the way until the coachee has gained what they want from coaching.

The single session and one-at-a-time mindset and mode of delivery

It should be clear by now that Single-Session Coaching and One-At-A-Time Coaching are not *approaches* to coaching since SSC/OAATC can be practised in a variety of ways. Thus, if they are not *approaches* then what are they? They are best seen as a *mindset* or an attitude to coaching and/or as a *mode of delivery* of coaching.

The single-session and one-at-a-time mindset

The SSC/OAATC mindset can be seen as comprising a number of perspectives that SSC/OAATC coaches bring to the work (Young, 2018):

- They are clear about the nature of SSC/OAATC with potential coachees before making SSC/OAATC contracts.
- They approach the first session 'as if' it could be the last.
- They explore what each coachee wants to walk away with at the end of the session at hand (rather than the usual question of what the coachee wants from a course of coaching).
- They prioritise what to focus on – negotiated between coachee and coach but largely coach led.
- They check in at various points throughout the session to ensure the work is on track.
- They seek to discover their coachees' internal strengths and external resources and encourage them to use these strengths/resources during the session and beyond.

- They work driven by the idea "what would I want to share with this coachee if I never see them again?"
- They provide resources and clarify next steps.

SSC/OAATC as a mode of delivery

There are various ways in which coaching can be delivered. In individual coaching where the coachee is coached by a professionally trained coach, contracts can be ongoing or time-limited. Coaching can occur in groups or be done by peers working with one another where both occupy the role of coach and coachee alternately. As well as a mindset, then, SSC/OAATC can be seen as a mode of coaching delivery (Young, 2018). Most often SSC/OAATC, as a coaching mode, is entered into with the expressed intention of seeing if the coachee can be helped in one session. If not, more coaching is available. However, following the Single-Session Therapy work at the Bouverie Centre, Melbourne, Australia, it is possible to organise a coaching agency where a single session is offered to everyone in the first instance. If the coachee is helped in one session, then they stop there. If not they come back for a second session. However, at the end of the first session, it may become clear that the coachee is better served by a different form of coaching, e.g. ongoing coaching, group coaching or peer coaching which can be provided by the agency. In this case, they will be referred to this different service.

Why SSC/OAATC?

Why would a coach offer SSC/OAATC and why would a coachee seek it? There are basically two reasons: i) positive and ii) pragmatic. In this chapter, I explain the reasons for SSC/OAATC and the positives of offering, seeking and sampling this form of coaching.

Positive reasons for SSC/OAATC

In this section, I will assume that the main reasons for offering and seeking SSC/OAATC are positive rather than pragmatic.

Positive reasons for offering SSC/OAATC

Not all coaches are drawn to single-session work. Those who are, see the benefits of what it has to offer.

Thus, in *single-session development-focused coaching*, these coaches see that when both coach and coachee have a single coaching session to do their work, this time-frame concentrates both of their minds and helps them to be focused on what the coachee wants to achieve and how this can be done. Although all the work is not done in the session, the coach helps the coachee to develop a plan to get the work done by themself later. Furthermore, the coach believes that the coachee has the internal resources to get the job done and facilitates the coachee to do so as well as encouraging the coachee to use appropriate external resources.

In *single-session problem-focused coaching*, these coaches again hold the view that the coach and coachee both working together can help the coachee identify a potential solution to their problem (or coaching-related obstacle) and develop a plan to implement it in a single session while drawing upon relevant internal strengths and utilising external resources.

Positive reasons for seeking SSC/OAATC

Coachees who are drawn towards SSC/OAATC tend to be so because it resonates with their own values and/or personality structure. For example, coachees who value self-help are likely to seek SSC/OAATC because it is consistent with this value. Also, coachees who have an autonomous personality will tend to seek out SSC/OAATC because they will want to take what a coach has to offer and apply it to their own life for themself.

Other positive reasons for seeking SSC/OAATC include:

Sampling coaching. If you are buying a new car, it is unlikely that you will do so without taking it for a test drive. Similarly, if a person is interested in becoming a coachee, but is shopping around to see what is on offer, then having a single session with a coach may help them make their mind up (Dryden, 2017b). Here the coach would agree to coach the person for a single session so that the latter can get a 'feel' of what it is like to be coached by the former and how the coach works. In this situation, the person may have single 'sample' sessions with a number of coaches. Such a sample session may, of course, be the first session that the person may have with the practitioner that they choose to have as their coach for a longer-term contract. Sometimes it happens that the coachee gets what they were looking for from a 'sample' session and no longer requires coaching at least for the time being.

In Chapter 2, I mentioned the case of Bettany who while being trained to become a GROW coach (Whitmore, 2017) developed an interest in Rational Emotive Behavioural Coaching (Dryden, 2018a) and wanted to get a 'feel' of what the approach was like in action rather than just reading about it. With that objective in mind, I agreed to a one-session contract with Bettany on the understanding that she brings a genuine issue that she wants coaching help with.

Volunteering to be coached. When coaches give training workshops on their way of working, often they are prepared to demonstrate this. When I do so, I stress that it is important that the volunteer has a genuine development-based issue or a problem/coaching-based obstacle they want to address. In doing so, we both know that this will be our only opportunity to work together and consequently this will be a single coaching session. In Chapter 2, I mentioned the case of Adriana who volunteered for a single session of coaching to address an obstacle that she was encountering in her ongoing development-based coaching. I have done numerous such demonstrations, and they are very often sufficient for the person (see Dryden 2018b, 2019b).

Pragmatic reasons for SSC/OAATC

In this section, I will assume that the main reasons for offering and seeking SSC/OAATC are pragmatic rather than positive.

Pragmatic reasons for offering SSC/OAATC

In counselling and psychotherapy, agencies often introduce single-session and one-at-a-time therapeutic work to address their lengthening waiting list problem. For example, counselling services in higher education in the UK often do reduce waiting lists by delivering counselling based on One-At-A-Time (OAAT) Therapy (Dryden, 2019a, 2019c). Such agencies would probably not introduce SST/OAAT if their standard mode of counselling delivery produced no waiting lists.

The 'waiting list' problem may exist in coaching when sponsoring organisations pay for their employees to have ongoing coaching or even time-limited coaching. There are two ways of dealing with the waiting list here. First, the sponsoring organisation may limit ongoing or time-limited coaching to certain employees. This may create a divided 'have' and 'have not' workforce which will probably be counterproductive with respect to staff morale. The second way of responding to the waiting list problem is to 'cap' the number of coaching sessions so that all may have 'some' coaching. SSC/OAATC can be offered here if its strengths are marketed well and it does not appear to potential coachees that they are being offered an inferior product. In particular, One-At-A-Time Coaching (OAATC) with its emphasis on coachee reflection-digestion-action-letting time pass before an additional coaching session may be scheduled perhaps represents the best solution here since it addresses the waiting list problem and offers additional coaching sessions with time to put into practice what has been learned from the previous session. Indeed, quite a few coachees who have coaching based on OAATC only attend one session and are happy with what they have taken away from that session.

Pragmatic reasons for seeking SSC/OAATC

People who seek SSC/OAATC for pragmatic reasons tend to have limited time and/or financial resources to spend on coaching. Often these coachees are sponsored by their employing organisation but are not given sufficient time to attend coaching sessions or sufficient funds to pay for them. They still want coaching and will accept a contract for SSC/OAATC because they think they can derive benefit from it.

Other pragmatic reasons for coachees seeking SSC/OAATC include:

Geographical reasons. Here the coachee lives far from the coach and does not want coaching by Skype or another similar platform. So, the coachee books a coaching session one at a time whenever they are in the same geographical location as the coach.

Cost. For some coachees the cost of longer-term coaching is prohibitive, and they can only afford to pay for coaching one session at a time.

Time. Some coachees may benefit from a longer-term contract with a coach but cannot spare the time to devote to having the sessions they would ideally need. Rather than have no coaching such people will book for coaching one session at a time when their busy schedule allows them to do so.

While I have considered positive and pragmatic reasons for offering and seeking SSC/OAATC separately, I do wish to stress that such reasons may operate together rather than separately and when they do act together they can serve as a powerful force for change in both developmental-focused SSC/OAATC and problem-focused SSC/OAATC.

Development-focused SSC/OAATC

In this book, I discuss two forms of coaching: a) development-focused coaching where the emphasis is on fostering coachee development and b) problem-focused coaching where the coachee has a problem that they are seeking coaching help with or they are experiencing an obstacle to progress in development-focused coaching which they need to address in order to resume the pursuit of their development-based objective. In this chapter, I will discuss development-focused SSC/OAATC while in the following chapter, I will discuss problem-focused SSC/OAATC.

As the name implies, development-focused coaching's emphasis is on helping coachees to develop themselves. By development, I mean where coachees seek to get the most out of themselves in nominated life domains (e.g. work, relationships, personal life). When the single-session or one-at-a-time coach does development-focused coaching, they will bring the skills and insights of SSC/OAATC to this form of coaching. What follows is when the coach does this.

Helping the coachee to identify and work with one meaningful objective[1]

In SSC/OAATC, there is only time to work on one meaningful objective in one nominated life domain.

What are the features of a well-chosen development-based objective

A well-chosen development-based objective has a number of features:

- It has a direction
- It may be ongoing (thus it may not have a final end-point)
- When it does have a final end-point, this point needs to be maintained
- A development-based objective is broad with specific referents

Conditions that facilitate the pursuit of a development-based objective

When working with a coachee to select a meaningful development-based objective, it is vital for the coach to help the coachee to keep in mind the following conditions that facilitate their pursuit of a development-based objective:

- It has intrinsic rather than extrinsic importance[2]
- It tends to be based on a value that is important to the coachee
- It involves tasks that have intrinsic merit for the coachee
- The objective should be one that the coachee is prepared to integrate into their life. This means:
  - They can devote time to pursuing it on a regular basis
  - They have ready access to any resources they need to pursue the objective
  - It is not going to clash with other priorities that they have in their life
- It involves active rather than passive desires
- It is an objective for which the coachee is prepared to make sacrifices to achieve

Helping the coachee to design and implement an action plan

Once the coachee has selected a meaningful, development-based objective, the next step is for the coach to help them to design and implement an action plan geared to helping them reach the objective.

Designing the action plan

When helping the coachee to devise an action plan with respect to reaching their developmental-based objective, it is important for the SSC/OAATC coach to take the following steps, the order of which is to be determined between coach and coachee:

- Help the coachee to set criteria for the achievement of their development-based objective. These should be as specific as possible.
- Help the person to set a clear signpost that tells them that they are on the way to achieving their objective. If possible, the coachee needs to leave the session confident that they will be able to reach the signpost.
- Help the coachee to list the actions that they need to take to reach the signpost and, if possible, their objective.
- Help the coachee to prepare a realistic time schedule to achieve the signpost and, if possible, the objective.
- Help the coachee to use their strengths and other helping resources in the service of reaching their signpost and later their objective.
- Ensure that the coachee can integrate the action plan into their life.
- Help the coachee to identify in advance possible obstacles that they may encounter during the process of working towards the signpost and, if necessary, the objective.

Implementing the action plan

A significant difference between single-session development-focused coaching and longer-term development-focused coaching is that in the former, the coachee will not be able to report back on their experiences in implementing the action plan which may include dealing with difficulties with its implementation[3]. All the coach can do in the single session is to encourage the person to project forward and picture themself implementing the plan and predicting what obstacles might be encountered which may then be dealt with in the single session.

In one-at-a-time development-focused coaching, where the contract is that the coachee may return for further sessions of coaching organised one session at a time after they have had the opportunity to get the most from the previous session, the coachee's experiences with implementing their action plan can be discussed with the coach.

Helping the coachee to monitor the implementation of their action plan

In OAATC, the coach can help the coachee develop a system to monitor their progress towards their signpost and the objective itself. There is no set way of doing this, and the coach can encourage the coachee to develop their own monitoring system (Dryden, 2018c).

Understanding and dealing with actual obstacles to coachee progress

In OAATC, the coachee may come back and deal with actual obstacles that they encounter when implementing their action plan. If this obstacle is a practical one, then the coach and coachee can use practical problem-solving methods (Dryden, 2018c). However, if the obstacle is emotionally based, then coach and coachee can use insights and practices from problem-focused SSC/OAATC which I discuss in the following chapter.

Problem-focused SSC/OAATC

Again, as the name implies, problem-focused coaching's emphasis is on helping coachees to address problems. In this book, I will concentrate on emotional problems – either in the guise of obstacles to progress in development-focused coaching or in their own right[1]. Cavanagh's (2005) suggestions concerning what emotional problems can be usefully tackled in coaching are particularly useful for problem-focused SSC/OAATC. Here are his criteria:

- The emotional problem is of recent origin or occurs intermittently
- The responses of the coachee to the adversity are distressing to the person but lie within a mild to moderate range of distress
- The coachee's emotional problem is limited to a particular situation or aspect of the person's life
- The coachee is not defensive with respect to the problem
- The person is open to address and change the problem.

My own view is that an emotional problem occurs when a person feels emotionally stuck in the face of some kind of adversity. The role of the SSC/OAATC is to help them get unstuck. When the single-session or one-at-a-time coach does problem-focused coaching, they will again bring the skills and insights of SSC/OAATC to this form of coaching. What follows is when the coach does this.

Helping the coachee to focus on their problem

When the coachee has a problem, then it is important to help them to focus on it. This means that the coach only asks the person for information that is relevant to the problem. In keeping focused on the coachee's problem, then the coach may need to interrupt the coachee. The best way of doing so is to explain why such interruptions may be necessary and to ask the coachee's permission to do so. When interrupting the coachee, the coach needs to do so with tact.

If the coachee mentions more than one problem, the coach needs to help the person to select the one that is most problematic for the person or the one that is causing the biggest obstacle to the coachee's progress to their development-based objective. This is known as the target problem.

Helping the coachee to understand their target problem

Once the coachee's target problem has become the agreed focus, then the coach and coachee need to understand this problem and what factors are operating to maintain its existence. The coach will ask questions to help them both assess the problem. This assessment will be an amalgam of both the coach's and the coachee's respective views of the problem and related factors. Amongst others these are the features of the problem that are identified:

- The adversity that the coachee is most disturbed about
- The coachee's main disturbed emotion
- How the coachee thinks about the adversity
- How the coachee responds behaviourally to the adversity
- Factors that serve to maintain the problem
- What steps the coachee has taken to solve the problem and the outcome of these steps

Helping the coachee to set a problem-related goal[2]

Once the coachee's target problem has been understood, the next stage is for the coach to help the coachee to set a realistic problem-related goal. This goal may involve the coachee bypassing the problem-related adversity or one that involves the person facing this adversity and dealing with it effectively. Harry came to SSC/OAATC with a procrastination problem. He wanted to learn new skills at work but kept putting off learning them. His procrastination was based on his fear of having his efforts criticised. If his goal bypassed his adversity (i.e. being criticised), it would focus on his avoidant behaviour and specify taking action. If his goal involved facing the adversity, it would focus on being criticised and nominate a constructive response to this adversity.

Helping the coachee to address their problem and find a potential solution

After a goal has been agreed, the next step is for the coach to help the person address the problem. In my view, this is best done by helping the person deal with the adversity at the heart of their problem until they find a potential solution to the problem, one which will help them to achieve their problem-related goal as shown in Figure 8.1.

Helping the coachee to develop an action plan which will frame the pursuit of the problem-related goal

In developing an action plan to deal with the problem and help the person to reach their problem-related goal, it is important that the person implements the solution in the face of the adversity. Thus, in

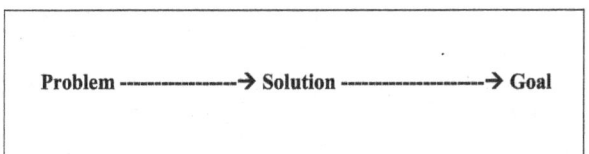

Figure 8.1

Harry's case, his potential solution was to reframe the meaning of criticism, and he planned to practise this solution while giving his work to his tutor. In doing so, he would work to achieve his goal to be bothered but not overwhelmed by such criticism. His action plan involved him first practising his solution in imagery before giving in work directly to his tutor. In imagery, he began by thinking that the criticism was mild, then moderate and then finally severe. Then he resolved to hand in his assignments on time. In the session, his coach helped Harry to practise the solution by role-playing his boss first giving mild, then moderate and finally severe criticism while Harry practised his solution by verbalising his reframe.

If the coach and coachee have only one session, then as in development-focused coaching, they will not have a chance to deal with the coachee's experiences in implementing the action plan. However, particularly in OAATC, this can be done if the coachee decides to return for more sessions.

Helping the coachee to anticipate and plan to deal with potential obstacles to the implementation of the action plan

If there is time in the single session, then it is important for the coach to help the coachee to think about what obstacles they might encounter in implementing the action plan and then problem-solve possible solutions. In OAATC such work tends to be done once the obstacle has been encountered and the coachee becomes stuck in the face of its existence. At this point, the person returns for a session to get unstuck.

The working alliance in SSC/OAATC

In my view, any helping endeavour needs to be considered as an alliance between helper and helpee. This is true whether the intervention in therapy-focused or coaching-focused. Working alliance theory is based on the pioneering work of Ed Bordin (1979) who took the psychoanalytic concept of the 'working alliance', updated it and showed the generalizability of his updated framework. In what follows I will use my reformulation of Bordin's (1979) tripartite model of the working alliance (Dryden, 2011, 2017b). This posits that there are four components of the alliance: bonds, views, goals and tasks.

Bonds

The coach needs to build a good *bond* between them and their coachee and do so as quickly as possible. In my view, the best way that the coach can do this is to demonstrate to the client that they genuinely want to help the person as quickly as possible to develop themself or to solve their problem, but to do so without rushing the coachee. In doing so, the coach encourages the coachee to participate actively in the process and to set the coaching agenda.

Views

It is important that the coach and coachee share the same *view* concerning the nature and purpose of SSC/OAATC. In particular, the coachee needs to understand if more coaching sessions are possible after the first session and this needs to be made explicit by the coach and agreed to by the coachee. In addition, in development-focused SSC/OAATC, the coach and coachee need to agree concerning which area of the coachee's life they are going to focus on in the session and in problem-focused SSC/OAATC there needs to be a similar agreement concerning the nature of the coachee's target problem or coaching-related obstacle that needs to be addressed.

Goals

It is important for the coach and coachee to agree concerning the direction of the coaching enterprise. In development-focused SSC/OAATC, it is important that they agree concerning what the coachee's development-based objectives are and in problem-focused SSC/OAATC there needs to be agreement on the coachee's problem-based goals.

Tasks

It is important that the coachee can make sense of any *tasks* that the coach suggests that they use and can see the relevance of doing them to achieving their development-based objective or problem-based goal. Given the nature of SSC/OAATC, it is vital that any suggested task is simple to understand and implement even though doing so may not be easy.

Research

While there is no research currently on the working alliance and SSC/OAATC, research in therapy shows clients who benefit from Single-Session Therapy report that they had a better working alliance with their therapists than those who did not benefit (Simon, Imel,

Ludman & Steinfeld, 2012). Extrapolating from this, it is crucial, therefore, that the single-session and one-at-a-time coach needs to pay attention to the working alliance between them and their coachee.

Many coaches are sceptical of the value of SSC because they think that they will not be able to form a strong enough working alliance with their coachees for them to do any useful work in the session with them. I hope the points I have made and Simon et al.'s (2012) research show that this is not the case.

What makes a good SSC/OAATC coach and coachee?

In this chapter, I will give my views on what makes a good SSC/OAATC coach and which coachees are likely to benefit most from SSC/OAATC.

What makes a good SSC/OAATC coach?

Not all coaches can see the value of SSC/OAATC, and of those who can, not all of them will make good SSC/OAATC coaches. Perhaps the most important characteristic that a good SSC/OAATC coach has is a conviction of what can be achieved when the coach and coachee set out with the intention of helping the coachee get the most from the session. In addition, here is a list of the characteristics that good SSC/OAATC coaches have:

- They have a realistic outlook about what can be achieved in SSC/OAATC and can help coachees share this outlook
- They can engage with coachees quickly
- They are ready to get down to work straight away
- They are active in the coaching process while encouraging their coachees' active participation
- They can help coachees focus quickly and stay focused
- They help coachees, in problem-focused SSC/OAATC, to differentiate between problems that can be changed and problems that can't be changed and to focus on the former (Talmon, 1993)
- They encourage coachees to identify their strengths, to use these in the session and to plan to apply them after the session

- They help coachees to identify and address the obstacles effectively to their development-based objectives and problem-based goals
- They can tolerate not having information about coachees
- They are flexible in thinking and practice and have a pluralistic outlook. Thus they can suggest a variety of activities for coachees to consider to help them achieve their problem-related goal or development-related objective
- They are able to think quickly on their feet
- They can move with relative ease from the specific to the general and back again

Which coachees are likely to benefit most from SSC/OAATC?

Not all coachees want very brief coaching, and of those who do, not all would benefit from SSC/OAATC. Here is a list of characteristics that help coachees to get the most from SSC/OAATC:

- They have a realistic outlook about what can be achieved in SSC/OAATC
- They have a clear idea of what they want to achieve from development-focused SSC/OAATC and are ready to get down to work immediately
- In problem-focused SSC/OAATC, they can quickly identify their target problem or obstacle to progress in development-focused coaching and are ready to address this problem/obstacle quickly
- In problem-focused SSC/OAATC, they can focus on available solutions which they are prepared to implement immediately (Talmon, 1993)
- They are prepared to be as actively engaged as possible in the process
- They can identify their strengths and can see how they can utilise them to achieve their problem-based goal or development-based objective

- They can focus and clearly and explicitly articulate their target problem and related goal in problem-focused SSC/OAATC and their objective in development-focused SSC/OAATC
- They are prepared to practise goal-related or objective-related activities in the session
- They are prepared immediately to put into practice in their life what they learn from the session

Misconceptions of SSC/OAATC

In this chapter, I consider a number of misconceptions that some people hold about SSC/OAATC when they are first introduced to it and that others hold even before they have been introduced to it! Having listed each misconception, I set out to correct it.

SSC/OAATC is a specific approach to coaching

In Chapter 5, I discussed the position that there are two ways of best viewing SSC/OAATC, as a mindset, an attitude towards coaching that influences practice and as a mode of delivering coaching services.

Consequently, SSC/OAATC is not a coaching approach in the way that cognitive-behavioural coaching (Neenan, 2018) or the GROW model (Whitmore, 2017) are approaches to coaching. As both a mindset and a mode of coaching delivery it can be practised by coaches from any approach to coaching.

SSC/OAATC replaces other modes of coaching delivery

It is essential to make clear that SSC/OAATC is best seen as occupying a vital place in a range of coaching services available within a coaching agency's service provision. It is not designed to replace such services, and nobody in the SSC/OAATC community would argue that it should be offered to and used with everybody seeking development-focused coaching or problem-focused coaching.

SSC/OAATC is a quick fix

This is a misconception that applies particularly to problem-focused SSC/OAATC and is also made about Single-Session Therapy (Dryden, 2019d).

The term 'quick fix' means something that *seems* to be a *fast* and *easy solution* to a *problem* but is, in *fact*, not very good or will not last *long*. This is not what SSC/OAATC coaches attempt to do when working with their coaches' problems or coaching-related obstacles. Instead, these coaches strive to work with coaches to find a durable solution to a problem or obstacle or to help them take steps that will lead to such a solution.

SSC/OAATC is used to save money

Budget holders may be attracted to SSC/OAATC because they see it as a way of reducing costs. While this may be true in certain situations, it neglects the fact that SSC/OAATC has particular potency when practised well. Thus, even if a person is restricted to a single session of coaching much can be achieved from that session if both coach and coachee think that it can and act on that understanding.

SSC/OAATC restricts access to coaching

The basic principle behind SSC/OAATC is that the coach helps the coachee get the most out of a coaching session on the understanding that it *may* be the only session that they have. It is possible to offer coachees one session of coaching which is not informed by the principle of helping them get the most out of the session. This would be a double penalty – restricting the coachee to one session and not helping them to get the most out of that session.

The way SSC/OAATC is generally practised, further sessions are possible, usually booked one-at-a-time rather than, for example, booked weekly well into the future, unless this is what the coach and coachee have contracted for. In an organisation where due to budgetary constraints, coachees cannot have ongoing coaching, then SSC/OAATC can be offered so that all who want it may have and benefit from some coaching. Here, if both coach and coachee share the SSC/OAATC mindset much can be achieved. Thus, access to coaching is not restricted, but it is tempered by the needs of all in that organisation who want coaching so that nobody has to wait longer than they need to for it.

SSC/OAATC is coaching speeded-up

Some people think that SSC/OAATC is like 'coaching speeded up' where the coach attempts to cram a number of sessions into one session. This is not the case. In fact, if a coach attempts to do this, it often renders SSC/OAATC ineffective. A single session of coaching has its own process and has a beginning, a middle and an end (Hoyt, 2018). The coach does not try and 'shoehorn' a number of sessions into one but uses the time productively to help the coach to get the most out of that one session even though they may request another session later. Thus, an SSC/OAATC session is regarded as a whole, complete in itself (Talmon, 1990).

SSC/OAATC is easy because it involves one session

Some coaches think that ongoing coaching is complex and this may well be the case. Such coaches think that, by contrast, brief coaching is relatively easy, and by extension, SSC/OAATC is the easiest of them all. However, the reverse is probably the case. Given its brevity and focus, SSC/OAATC is quite difficult to practise, and SSC/OAATC coaches require high-level coaching skills to practise it well.

SSC/OAATC is for everyone

While SSC/OAATC can be helpful, it is indeed not for all coachees. There are coachees who want longer-term coaching and would not respond well to being offered a single session even if further sessions may be available and even if a compelling case for the use of SSC/OAATC is made.

Also, SSC/OAATC is not for all coaches. Some coaches think that it is necessary for them to carry out a full history and case formulation before they begin to coach. Clearly, these activities cannot be undertaken in SSC/OAATC, and such coaches would struggle to practise coaching when time is at a premium (Dryden, 2016).

It is neither a good idea to require coachees to have SSC/OAATC when it is not wanted, nor to mandate coaches to practise SSC/OAATC, particularly where their ideas and related skills are not consistent with the SSC/OAATC mindset (see Chapter 5). On the contrary, SSC/OAATC is best practised when coachees see the potential in it, and coaches rise to the challenge of helping willing and engaged coachees in the shortest possible period.

Part II

PRACTICE

Good practice in SSC/OAATC

In my view, good practice in SSC/OAATC is marked by flexibility and pluralism. In this chapter, which will serve as an overview of the practice of SSC/OAATC, I will outline the pluralistic foundations of SSC/OAATC before specifying elements of its good practice.

The pluralistic foundations of SSC/OAATC

In the pluralistic practice of SSC/OAATC, coaches show commitment to valuing diversity and suspicion of single, all-embracing 'truths' (see Dryden, 2018c). More specifically:

- They hold that there is no one absolute right way of understanding coachees and that different viewpoints are useful for different coachees
- They adhere to the view that there is no one right way of practising SSC/OAATC. Different coachees need different things, and therefore coaches need to have a broad practice repertoire
- They are more likely to resolve practical issues and dilemmas taking a 'both-and' perspective, rather than an 'either/or' one
- They acknowledge and celebrate clients' diversity and uniqueness
- They involve coachees fully throughout the SSC/OAATC process
- They understand coachees in terms of their strengths and resources as well as their areas of struggle
- They should ideally have an openness to multiple sources of knowledge on how to practise SSC/OAATC including research, personal experience, and theory

For more information about pluralistic coaching, I recommend that the interested reader consults Utry, Palmer, McLeod and Cooper (2019).

Good practice elements of SSC/OAATC

Having made the point that the practice of SSC/OAATC is flexible and pluralistic, there are certain agreed practical do's and don'ts. In this chapter, I will outline the elements of its good practice, and in the following chapter, I will outline what to avoid.

The SSC/OAATC coach is clear with the coachee about why they are here, what they can do and what they can't do

Unless the coachee understands that they are contracting for SSC/OAATC and what can be realistically expected from it, then the potency of the process will be diluted. Coach clarity on these points is crucial.

The SSC/OAATC coach engages the coachee quickly through the work

In both development-focused and problem-focused SSC/OAATC, it is vital for the coach to start work immediately and to engage the coachee through doing so.

The SSC/OAATC coach is prudently active

Unless the coachee indicates that they would value the coachee adopting a listening role, the coach needs to be prudently active. By this, I mean that they are active in addressing the person's development issue or target problem while also promoting coachee activity.

The SSC/OAATC coach is focused and helps the client stay focused

If the coachee is going to take away something meaningful from SSC/OAATC, then the coach will have to work with them to create a meaningful focus in the session. In development-focused coaching, the focus should be on the coachee's development-based objective and in problem-focused coaching it should be on the coachee's problem and related goal.

Once a relevant focus has been co-created by the coach and coachee, the coach needs to help the coachee stay focused throughout the session. If necessary, the coach tactfully interrupts the coachee having given a prior rationale for doing this and eliciting the client's agreement to do so.

In development-focused SSC/OAATC, the coach helps the coachee to identify and work with a personally meaningful objective

Such an objective will likely have a number of characteristics which I will discuss in Chapter 21.

In problem-focused SSC/OAATC, the coach helps the coachee to identify their target problem and work with a relevant goal

I will again discuss this further in Chapter 21.

If the coachee talks about the past, the SSC/OAATC coach bridges to the future whenever possible

Most coaching is future-oriented, and SSC/OAATC is no exception.

Whenever practicable, it is important for the SSC/OAATC coach to explain what they are doing

However, they should refrain from doing so obsessively.

The SSC/OAATC coach helps the coachee to identify their internal strengths and to make use of these strengths during SSC/OAATC

Many, but not all, single-session and one-at-a-time coaches hold that as time is at a premium in SSC/OAATC, all the coach can do is to harness the existing skills that the coachee has in their repertoire and encourage them to use these in the session to further their development or to address their problem. Other coaches would agree, in part, but also argue that the coachee can be taught new skills in the session which they can use after the session. In this latter case, the coachee should be encouraged to practise these skills in the session.

The SSC/OAATC coach helps the coachee to identity and use where appropriate the external resources that are available to them to aid the coaching process

In particular, it is useful for the coachee to nominate people in their life that could support them as they go through the coaching process. This is particularly relevant in SSC/OAATC since the coachee will be working by themself after the single session or between sessions contracted one at a time, and the assistance provided by supportive people can make all the difference. As the saying goes, "Only you can do it, but you don't have to do it alone".

The SSC/OAATC coach helps the coachee to identify previous attempts at furthering their development or solving similar or related problems

In doing so, the coach encourages the coachee to use and build on successful strategies and discontinue the use of unsuccessful strategies.

The SSC/OAATC coach helps the coachee to identify and use their preferred learning style during and after the session

The SSC/OAATC coach makes liberal use of questions

In doing so, it is vital that the coach gives the coachee time to answer their questions and ensures that the coachee actually answers the questions they are asked.

At times during the session, the SSC/OAATC coach will make a substantive point, and when they do so, it is important that they check to ensure the coachee's understanding

The SSC/OAATC coach will be mindful that the coachee may have some doubts, reservations and objections (DROs) about an aspect of the coaching process including those that may be expressed non-verbally

Once the coach has helped the coachee identify the DRO, then they help them consider it and respond to it.

The SSC/OAATC coach looks for ways to make an emotional impact

Given that the coach and coachee may only be meeting for one session, it is important that the coachee is appropriately emotionally engaged in the session. However, too much emotion and the coachee will not process information and too little emotion, and their learning will be theoretical. Given this, the coach should look for ways of engaging the coachee in an emotionally relevant conversation[1]. Having said this, the coach should not push to create an emotional impact, as the more they do so, the less likely it is to occur.

The SSC/OAATC coach aims to help the coachee to take one meaningful point from the session and to develop a plan to implement this point (Keller & Papasan, 2012)

Given the brevity of SSC/OAATC, the coach needs to guard against the tendency to overload the coachee with tips, skills and strategies to take forward on their own. Such overload generally results in the coachee not taking away anything of substance from the session. To guard against this, the coach might ask the coachee from the outset, "If you could only take away one thing from the session what do you hope that might be?" The answer might serve as a focus of the work to be done in the session. Once the point has been identified, then the coach can discuss a possible action plan to achieve it.

The SSC/OAATC coach encourages the coachee to practise a core 'take-away' in the session if possible

In problem-focused coaching, the coach and coachee work together to find a solution to the client's problem or coaching-related obstacle. If possible, it is beneficial for the coachee to practise this solution in the session before implementing it in a relevant situation. Such in-session practice might involve the coachee engaging in role-play, chair work or imagery (see Dryden 2019c).

In development-focused coaching, the coachee might be helped to practise an important skill in the session before doing so in life.

The SSC/OAATC coach periodically uses capsule summaries to keep the process on track and the momentum going

This is an important practice as it is easy for both coach and coachee to drift away from the agreed focus as their conversation unfolds.

Just before the end of the session, the SSC/OAATC coach encourages the coachee to summarise the session and what they are going to take away from it

It is vital that the coachee does this rather than the coach because it demonstrates what the highlight of the session has been for the coachee. However, the coach might make explicit any crucial points that the coachee has missed, if they think it necessary.

After the summary, the SSC/OAATC coach ties up any loose ends with the coachee by asking them if there is anything they wish to raise before the session ends

A good question here is, "When you get home and you think about the session, is there anything you wished you had told me or asked me during the session that you didn't? If so, what would that be?"

The SSC/OAATC coach discusses the possibility of another session or sessions with the coachee

By now, it should be clear that SSC/OAATC involves the possibility of more than one session. Thus, at the end of the session, the coach develops criteria with the coachee concerning access to further coaching sessions.

The SSC/OAATC coach agrees with the coachee a date for a follow-up evaluation meeting

This enables the coach to obtain both outcome and service evaluations.

Having outlined good practice in SSC/OAATC in the next chapter, I will discuss what coaches should ideally try to avoid in SSC/OAATC.

What not to do in SSC/OAATC

As well as the elements of good practice in SSC/OAATC listed and discussed in Chapter 12, it is also important for coaches to be aware of what practices to *avoid*, if at all possible, even though many of the items discussed here constitute the opposite of these good practices.

Practice elements to avoid in SSC/OAATC

The SSC/OAATC coach should not take an elaborate history

If the coach does so, this may take up the entire session and they won't have time to do any development-focused or problem-focused coaching with the coachee.

The SSC/OAATC coach should not let the coachee talk in an unfocused, general way

While certain coaches clients may gain benefit from a single session of unfocused exploration, most won't.

The SSC/OAATC coach should not spend too much time in passive, listening mode

The exception to this is when a client says that the best way the coach can help them is just to listen. However, this is a rare occurrence, and thus the coach in general needs to be active in their interaction with the coach. This does not preclude listening and understanding, but these activities are a prelude to intervention.

The SSC/OAATC coach should not strive to develop rapport independent of the task of the session

In SSC/OAATC, the coach showing a coachee that they are keen to help the coachee as quickly as possible is perhaps the best way to strengthen the coaching bond.

The SSC/OAATC coach should not assess where not relevant

The coach's assessment practices in SSC/OAATC should be driven by the coachee's objective in development-focused coaching and their goal in problem-focused coaching.

The SSC/OAATC coach should not carry out an elaborate case conceptualisation

Recently, it has been argued that the practice of coaching will be enhanced if the coach develops a 'case' formulation. This involves the collection of relevant information about the coachee, what they want to achieve, how they have already gone about achieving it, the role of stakeholders in the coaching work to be done amongst others (Lane & Corrie, 2009). However relevant this information might be in ongoing coaching, there is insufficient time in SSC/OAATC for such a formulation to be done.

The SSC/OAATC coach should not assume that the coachee knows what they are doing or why they are doing it

Explicitness and clarity are hallmarks of good SST/OAAT.

The SSC/OAATC coach should not rush the client

When I first became interested in the fields of Single-Session Coaching and Therapy and One-At-A-Time Coaching and Therapy, I thought that in order to get the job done, the practitioner needed to rush through the process. Having had quite a lot of experience in working very briefly with people, particularly with those who volunteer for demonstrations of therapy or coaching in front of a professional audience where sessions last for no more than 30 minutes, I know that this is not the case (Dryden, 2018b, 2019b). Consequently, I now think that the coach who paces themself and works at the coachee's pace will get far more done in a single session than a coach who rushes themself and their coachee through the process.

Placing SSC/OAATC in context

In the first part of this book, I discussed the distinctive theoretical features of SSC/OAATC, while in this part, I am focusing on its distinctive practical features. However, no matter how skilful an SSC/OAATC coach is, the effectiveness of their practice also depends on how well this mode of coaching delivery has been contextualised. Thus, for a person to give their informed consent to SSC/OAATC, they first have to understand it, and for them to understand it, it needs to have been placed in a suitable context.

SSC/OAATC as described on coaches' websites

Most coaches who work independently have websites where they outline their services. Coaches who mention SSC/OAATC services on their websites also describe other coaching services. This helps the person who is thinking about seeking coaching decide if they want to seek coaching from a particular coach and what coaching service would suit them best. Here are two examples of how coaches describe their SSC/OAATC services.

Example 1

Single Session Coaching is available when you have a burning topic that needs one session of laser-focused coaching to make a difference.

- Email or call me to set up a 90-minute coaching session on one issue.
- Be prepared for the session with a clear, focused, single topic for coaching, and a brief description of your current situation.
- Be open to engaging in direct, powerful questions.
- Know that you will end the session with deeper clarity, an inquiry for thoughtful consideration, and a self-chosen action step to begin the process of change[1].

Example 2

In this 1-hour transformative session, we will dive into the biggest issue you are currently facing in your life or business. We will get to the heart of the beliefs you are carrying around, identifying how they are stopping you from creating what it is you desire, work on healing the root cause, and develop practices for new habits to support you in moving forward in your life. You will receive homework and follow-up email access to ensure that the session is providing long-term impact[2].

SSC/OAATC as described to employees in an organisation

When SSC/OAATC coaching is offered to members of an organisation, it is usually because the organisation either does not have the funds to offer longer-term coaching or chooses not to do so. In these circumstances, it is vital that the organisation explains why SSC/OAATC is being offered and what can be achieved from this mode of coaching delivery. Here is an example of how this might be done. I have assumed that the following announcement was made by the organisation's HR department.

Example 3

The organisation has decided to offer all those employees who want it an opportunity to have a coaching session with a professional coach free of charge. If you want to develop yourself in a specific area of your work or you have a problem that you would like help with then please email Sally in HR. All coaching sessions are confidential. You will get the most from the session if you are clear about what you want to achieve from it. When you and your coach work together with the intention of dealing with the issue in one session, then this is often the result. If you need a further session, this may be possible too and your coach will discuss this with you at the end of your session.

SSC/OAATC as a gateway

When coaching is provided internally within an organisation there are a number of ways in which coaching delivery could be organised. One way of doing so is to offer a single session of coaching to everyone who requests coaching, with the understanding that for some this session will be sufficient, but for others, it won't be. For this latter group, other modes of coaching delivery will be more appropriate, and each person will get the type of coaching that best suits their needs. Jeff Young (2018) calls this the 'embedding process' where single-session services are embedded within the organisation so that coachees have additional coaching if they need and want it, whilst supporting the possibility that one session may be sufficient. In this way of organising coaching delivery, the single session is a gateway – the gate may be closed after the single session, or it may remain open for further coaching work to take place.

Responding to the first contact

Before I consider the issue of how an SSC/OAATC coach can respond to the first contact made by a potential coachee, I will first distinguish among the different roles a person can occupy with respect to seeking coaching help.

Garvin and Seabury (1997) argued that in social work there is an essential difference between a person occupying an 'applicant' role and one occupying the 'client' role. In the former case, the person has applied for help, but they and the social worker have not yet agreed to work together. When they agree to work together, it is after the 'applicant' has understood the nature of the help that they have applied for and has given their informed consent to proceed. Both the person and the worker understand their respective tasks and agree to carry these out. At this point, the 'applicant' has become a 'client'.

Four helping-seeking roles in coaching

Extending this analysis, I think that it is possible to distinguish among four roles that a person can occupy in the help-seeking process.

The 'explorer' role

When the person is occupying the 'explorer' role, they are interested in being coached and have embarked on an exploration of what is on offer. However, they have not yet made particular enquiries of any coach. Their exploration centres on reading about coaching and what is on offer, talking to people they know who have been coached and looking at the websites of coaches in general.

The 'enquirer' role

When the person is occupying the 'enquirer' role, they have formed an opinion about the type of coaching that might help them and have begun to make enquiries of particular coaches who practise in that way. Their enquiries may range from the technical, concerning more detailed information about how the coach practises, to the practical, concerning the coach's fees and availability, for example.

The 'applicant' role

When the person is occupying the 'applicant' role, they have a made a decision concerning the type of coaching that they think will help them and the coach whom they think is best suited to them and have asked the person if they will become their coach. In other words, the person has made an application for coaching help from their nominated coach.

The 'coachee' role

Extrapolating from the work of Garvin and Seabury (1997), whom I cited earlier, an applicant for coaching becomes a coachee when they have understood the nature of the coaching that they have applied for and have given their informed consent to proceed. This consent indicates, in my view, that both the coach and coachee understand their respective tasks and agree to carry these out.

Responding to the person's first contact

In this chapter, I will assume that the coach has a website and has SSC/OAATC listed on that site among other coaching services (and in some cases, therapy services) that they may offer[1]. When a person first contacts a coach, it will either be as an 'enquirer' or as an 'applicant'. I will deal with these two situations separately as they do require different responses.

Responding to the first contact from an 'enquirer'

Given that SSC/OAATC is listed on the coach's website, it is likely that the person has seen this and has some questions about SSC/OAATC and its applicability for them and their situation. One of the strengths of SSC/OAATC, at this point, is that it offers speed of response to potential coachees who are making these enquiries. In my own case, I answer my own phone and am happy to respond to any questions myself. If the person has left a message on my answer machine, then I undertake to phone them back as soon as possible. Here is what people who occupy the role of enquirer tend to ask or want to know:

They want to know more about what SSC/OAATC entails. I am happy to give more detail about SSC/OAATC, its goals and the fact that it is relevant to both the promotion of development and the resolution of common emotional problems or coaching-related obstacles.

They want to know if SSC/OAATC will be helpful to them. This is a difficult question to answer without finding out what the person is looking for and hoping to get from coaching. I tend not to get into this over the phone as it can lead to a lengthy conversation which is not appropriate with a person who is in the 'enquirer' role. However, I might suggest that as the best way of discovering if SSC/OAATC (or other modes of coaching delivery) is potentially helpful to the person they sign up for a single session of coaching, not necessarily with me, but with a coach with whom they resonate. I then ask the person to take time to reflect on that point and to contact me again if they would like a single session with me. If they do make contact with that request, they now occupy the role of an 'applicant'.

Responding to the first contact from an 'applicant'

As noted earlier, when an applicant makes contact with a coach, they have decided that they want to consult that coach and in this context, they want SSC/OAATC. In my own case, I ask the person what they are looking to gain from the session to determine whether that person's expectations are realistic. If the person's expectations are unrealistic, I explain why and encourage the person to reflect on this before contacting me again to proceed with a more realistic agenda. If the person's expectations are realistic, then their response also tells me if they are looking for development-focused SSC/OAATC or problem-focused SSC/OAATC. At this point, we are ready to move to the next stage of the coaching process which is contracting.

Contracting for SSC/OAATC

Much has been written on the topic of contracting in coaching (e.g. Bennett, 2008; Fielder & Starr, 2008; Lee, 2013)[1]. Contracting in SSC/OAATC takes place after the coach and applicant have notionally agreed to work together, but before the person can be considered to be in the role of 'coachee'. For this to happen, the applicant needs to give their consent to proceed. This is generally known as informed consent, and as the term suggests, it involves the applicant being informed by the coach about salient information to which they must give their consent. However, in my opinion, informed consent is best seen as a two-way process. In other words, the applicant also needs to inform the coach about salient information to which the coach needs to give their consent.

In this chapter, I will discuss the range of issues about which each party needs to inform the other before both give their consent. When this is done, SSC/OAATC can proceed.

The discussion prior to both parties giving their informed consent can be done face-to-face, by telephone or by Skype (or similar platform) and when informed consent is given it can either be formalised in writing[2] or agreed verbally.

Information provided by the coach

Here is the information the coach needs to give the applicant about their practice of SSC/OAATC.

PART II: PRACTICE

The nature of SSC/OAATC

It is crucial that the coach is very clear about how they practice SSC/OAATC given that there are a number of ways that it can be implemented (see Chapter 2). Here is what the coach needs to be clear about:

- *One session or the possibility of more.* If the SSC/OAATC only offers one session with no prospect of further sessions, then this needs to be clarified at the outset. The applicant may ask what happens, in this case, if they want further coaching and the coach needs to be ready with a clear answer to this question.
- *If further sessions are possible how these can be accessed.* Some coaches who practise SSC/OAATC say that they will endeavour to help the person get the coaching process underway in a single session, but that the coachee may have more sessions if needed. If this is the case, then the coach needs to be very clear with the applicant how such additional sessions can be accessed. Here is a list of areas that a coach may cover:

    1. Can the coachee book an additional session at the end of the single session or will they have to wait.
    2. If the coach offers SSC/OAATC where the 'reflect–digest–take action–let time pass' process is an integral part of their OAAT practice, then the coach needs to spell out what this means for the coachee. It usually means that the coachee will be asked to reflect on what they have learned from the session, digest this learning, act on what they have learned and then let time pass before requesting another session if they need one. My own practice here is to point out the value of the person engaging in this practice without being inflexible about this having to be done before scheduling the next appointment.
    3. If the coach practises One-At-A-Time Coaching rather than Single-Session Coaching their practice is based on the idea of offering a person one session per major coaching task or tasks. Thus, they might offer the coachee the first

session to get to know the person, find out what they want from coaching and set a development-based objective or a problem-based goal. Then they will encourage the coach to reflect on that work, digest it, etc. before they return for another session to deal with another significant task or set of tasks (e.g. action planning). Coaching proceeds one session at a time like this until the coachee has achieved what they came for. Once again, in the pre-contracting phase, the coach makes it clear that this is on offer.

Some coaches may offer only one or two of these types of SSC/OAATC while others may offer the full range. The more types of SSC/OAATC that a coach offers, the more they can tailor their information to the applicant's unique situation.

Other issues

There are a number of issues that the coach and applicant also have to agree on before informed consent can be given by both parties. This is the case with respect to all forms of coaching, and as they are not particular to SSC/OAATC, they fall outside the scope of this book. They are: i) The roles and responsibilities of all stakeholders; ii) Confidentiality and its limits and iii) Fees and the coach's cancellation policy[3].

Information provided by the applicant

There may also be information that the applicant needs to give the coach which may affect the coach's decision to take the person on as a coachee, and such information needs to be conveyed by the applicant at this point before the coach gives their informed consent to proceed. Thus, the coach may say to the applicant something like, "Is there any information you need me to know which may affect whether or not we decide to work with each other?" or "Do you have any questions for me the responses to which may affect your decision to have the single session with me?" This latter question often reveals an applicant's concerns which may preclude both parties giving informed consent if these concerns cannot be allayed.

Once all issues have been discussed, informed consent is given by both parties, and at this point, the applicant becomes a coachee.

Structuring the session effectively

It is vital that the SSC/OAATC coach is able to structure the session effectively. Otherwise, they will only do part of the work that they need to do to help the person get the most out of the session. Michael Hoyt (2000, 2018) has put forward one such structure. He argues that a single session has five phases. One phase is best seen as merging into the next, rather than as separate from it. However, in this chapter, I will discuss each phase separately.

Phase 1: The pre-session phase

At present, we do not have any walk-in coaching services. Thus, SSC/OAATC tends to be by appointment rather than by walk-in (Hoyt et al., 2018). This means that for both coach and coachee there is usually time between the point at which an appointment for the session is made and the beginning of the session itself. In the same way, as broadcasters eschew 'dead air', which is an "unintended period of silence that interrupts a broadcast during which no audio or video program material is transmitted"[1], SSC/OAATC sees this time as 'dead time' which could be filled with something that would help both the coach and the coachee prepare for the session so that the coachee gets the most from it. One way of doing this is for the coach and coachee to have a 'pre-session telephone conversation' during which the coach inducts the coachee into the SSC/OAATC process and sows the seeds for change by encouraging them to reflect on salient issues in preparation for the session (see Chapter 18). Hoyt (2000, 2018) refers to this phase as where induction and seeding occur.

If the SSC/OAATC dyad is not able to have such a conversation, then the coach may send the coachee some forms to complete and return before the session takes place. Such forms have a similar purpose to the pre-session telephone conversation. Table 17.1 presents one such form.

Table 17.1 A pre-session form for SSC/OAATC

Please complete this brief pre-coaching session form and return it to me before the session. Your responses will help us both to plan for our coaching session.

- With respect to the statements below, please indicate the two main ways in which I may be most helpful to you. Please put a tick (✓) to indicate each of these.
- With respect to statements below, please indicate the two strategies that I should not implement. Please put a cross (X) to indicate each of these.

1. Encouraging me to reflect on what is important to me	
2. Helping me to get more out of myself in one area of my life	
3. Helping me to focus on and solve a problem with which I feel emotionally stuck	
4. Helping me to understand and deal more constructively with people with whom I have a problem	
5. Helping me to focus on and deal constructively with an obstacle to my progess in coaching	
6. Helping me to maintain my progress towards personal development	
7. Discussing with me how I can change a problematic situation, assuming that the situation can be changed	
8. Helping me to adjust to a problematic situation, assuming that it can't be changed	
9. Encouraging me to take a few steps towards solving my problem and then letting me continue on my own	
10. Encouraging me to take a few steps towards my personal development and then letting me continue on my own	

To help you get the most from the coaching session, you may also want to answer the following questions briefly in the spaces provided.

1. What is the 'topic/issue' that is most important for us to focus on when we meet?

2. Why is this 'topic/issue' most important to you?

3. What helpful ideas have you had about this topic/issue?

4. When you think about this topic/issue, do you feel discouraged? If so, what do you feel discouraged about?

5. When we meet, what would you like to be the outcome of your coaching session?

6. How will you know that you have achieved that outcome?

© Windy Dryden & Jenny Forge, 2019

Phase 2: The early phase

In the early phase of SSC/OAATC, the coach may begin by linking the end of the pre-session conversation with the beginning of the session itself. Thus, if the coach suggested that the coachee should do something between the pre-session conversation and the session itself, then the coach could start with this topic. Also, since the pre-session conversation tends to stimulate much thought in the coachee, another way of beginning the session is by asking the coachee what they have been thinking about with respect to the session since the end of the pre-session conversation.

Another important task for the coach in the early phase is to firm up the coachee's objective in development-focused SSC/OAATC and their goal in problem-focused SSC/OAATC. Doing so gives the session a shared direction which is an integral part of alliance-building which as Hoyt (2000, 2018) has shown is a vital part of this phase.

Phase 3: The middle phase

It is in the middle phase that much of the focused work of SSC/OAATC is done. In development-focused SSC/OAATC, this concerns the formulation of an action plan where the coach helps the coachee to make sure that this is realistic and can be incorporated into the person's life. In problem-focused SSC/OAATC, this concerns the assessment of the problem or coaching-related obstacle[2] followed by the facilitation of a change-based refocusing and a discussion of possible solutions for change. This concludes with the selection of a solution most likely to succeed which is then rehearsed in the session.

Phase 4: The late phase

In development-focused SSC/OAATC, the late phase of the session is where discussion of ways to implement the action plan occur including the identification of possible obstacles and a plan to deal with these. In problem-focused SSC/OAATC, an action plan is developed with respect to the chosen solution, its implementation is discussed, and again possible obstacles are identified, and ways of dealing with these are discussed.

After this is done, a discussion occurs concerning the possibility of future sessions and how, if relevant, these can be accessed. In addition, loose ends are tied up, and plans for a follow-up are made, if appropriate.

Phase 5: The follow-through phase

Like the pre-session phase, the follow-up phase is not strictly part of the session itself but serves to evaluate it both from the perspective of the coachee ("What did I achieve?") and of the coach ("What did the coachee think of the service that I provided?"). As such it is an integral part of the work and needs to be seen as part of the SSC/OAATC process. This is another point at which the coachee can return for another session if needed.

Preparing for the session: The pre-session telephone conversation

In the field of therapy, there is a tradition in single-session work known as walk-in therapy (Slive & Bobele, 2011, 2014, 2018). Here, a client 'walks in' to an agency and sees a therapist straightaway at the point of need. In walk-in therapy, there is no opportunity for the therapist to help the client or themself to prepare for the session. Therapy begins the moment the client 'walks into' the session. At present, there is no equivalent to walk-in therapy in the coaching field. In other words, there is no formal area known as walk-in coaching[1]. Thus, before the session takes place in SSC/OAATC, the coach and the coachee have an opportunity to prepare themselves for it.

In this chapter, I will present a protocol that can be used by a coach with a coachee before that have met for the single session. This protocol can be used as a template for a discussion over the telephone – which I refer to as the 'pre-session telephone conversation' – or it can be sent to the coachee in the form of a questionnaire which the person can download, complete and return to the coach (see Table 17.1, Chapter 17). My preference is to use it as a template for a telephone conversation since this is interactive while the questionnaire is not. In the telephone conversation, I can modify the protocol based on the coachee's previous responses which cannot be done with a questionnaire. So, in this chapter, I will focus on preparing for the session by having a structured protocolled conversation with the coachee.

General questions

The questions that follow are suggestions, and the coach will use others as their conversation with the coachee unfolds.

"What made you decide that now is the right time for coaching?"

In SSC/OAATC, one of the important ingredients for change is 'coachee readiness for change'. Thus, it is important for the coach to understand why the person has sought coaching at the point when they have done so. Thus it makes a difference if the coach says something like, "Because I have a problem that I am ready to deal with", or "Because I feel ready to develop myself at work", than if they say something like, "Because my company announced that we were all entitled to one session of coaching, so I thought 'why not'?" As you can see, the first two coachees are 'ready' to initiate change while the third is not necessarily in that frame of mind. In such cases, I recommend following with a question such as, "Now you have decided to take up the company's offer, how would you like to use the session?"

"What issue do you want to address in the session?"

As we have seen, there are two forms of SSC/OAATC: development-focused SSC/OAATC (where the emphasis is on helping the coachee to promote their personal development in one area of their life) and problem-focused SSC/OAATC (where the emphasis is on helping the coachee to deal with an emotional problem or with an obstacle to progress in development-focused coaching). If it is not clear what type of coaching the coachee is looking for, then using a general term like 'issue' in the above question may reveal the answer. If it is already clear, then the coach can ask more focused questions such as:

"What area of personal development do you want to address in the session?" in development-focused SSC/OAATC.

"What problem do you want to address in the session?" in problem-focused SSC/OAATC.

At this point, it will be clear what type of SSC/OAATC the coachee needs, so the conversation proceeds in one of two ways.

Questions relevant to development-focused SSC/OAATC

In this section, I will assume that the person needs development-focused SSC/OAATC where they want help to develop themself in one chosen area of their life.

"Have you tried to develop yourself in this area before? If so, what did you do that was helpful and what was not helpful?"

In the session to come, time is at a premium (Dryden, 2016) and therefore the coach needs to know what to do that is helpful and what to avoid that is not helpful. Finding out what the person has already done with respect to the personal development issue is very useful in this context.

"What strengths and resiliency factors do you have as a person that you can use that might help you to develop yourself in your chosen area?"

It is an assumption of single-session work whether in the field of coaching or therapy that coachees/clients have strengths and resiliency factors that they can use in the single session and beyond and it is the role of coaches/therapists to help them to identify and use these strengths/resiliency factors. Examples of such strengths and resiliency factors might include: a positive outlook, spiritual convictions, a sense of hope, feelings of personal control, creativity, persistence and humour.

If the coachee struggles to answer this question, the following supplementary questions may be asked:

"What strengths and resiliency factors would those people who know you very well say that you have?"

"Imagine that you are being interviewed for a job that you really want and you are asked what strengths and resiliency factors you have as a person. How would you respond?"

"Who in your life could support you as you work towards developing yourself in your chosen area"?

There is an old adage which says, "I alone must do it, but I cannot do it alone" (Lonergan, 2012). Thus, it is useful to ask the coachee who could support them as they work towards their development-based objective. It may be that different people in the coachee's life support them in different ways and in this case, it is useful for the person to think of the concept of the team. Thus, if the coachee's name is Linda, she may be asked who she wants on 'Team Linda' and to ask them if they are prepared to be on the 'team'. It is useful for the coachee to give each person on their team a helping brief.

"Whom do you consider to be a role model who might directly or indirectly be helpful to you as you try to develop yourself in your chosen area?"

Such role models might include people whom the coachee knows personally (e.g. friends, family members and relatives) and inspirational figures whom the coachee knows of, but does not know personally. It is useful for the coach to discover in what way the role model may be helpful to the coach and to incorporate this information into interventions made during the session.

"What core values do you have that we might refer to in our work together as you develop yourself in your chosen area"?

The reason that I suggest that the coachee discovers their coachee's core values during the pre-session telephone contact is that doing so helps the coach to negotiate a development-based objective or problem-based goal since such objectives/goals that are underpinned by values are more likely to be pursued and achieved than objectives/goals that aren't (Eccles & Wigfield, 2002). Examples of values include honesty, loyalty, reliability and trustworthiness.

"What principles do you have that guide your life that might be relevant to you as you develop yourself in your chosen area?"

If the coachee struggles to understand what the coach means by a 'guiding principle', then the coach may give an example from their own life. When I explain this concept to a coachee, I tell them about a principle that guides my life that I remember being taught by my mother. This was, 'if you don't ask you don't get'. I remind myself of this principle whenever I am hesitant to go for something that I really want.

"How do you think I can best help you to develop yourself in your chosen area?"

While the coach may have a preferred way of helping a coach, one of the principles of SSC/OAATC is that the coach should endeavour to help a coachee in ways which the coachee deems to be helpful. If the coach has reservations about doing so these should be shared explicitly with the coachee and then discussed with any disagreements quickly resolved. If they cannot be resolved, then the contract between the two should be 'cancelled', and the coach should be referred to a coach who best matches their helping preferences.

Questions relevant to problem-focused SSC/OAATC

In this section, I will assume that the person needs problem-focused SSC/OAATC where they want help to deal with an emotional problem or address a coaching-related obstacle. In doing so, you will see that there are a number of questions that are common to both types of SSC/OAATC. Given that, I refer you to the relevant passages in the previous section.

"What are the factors (or circumstances) that have contributed to the problem (or coaching-related obstacle)?"

It is useful to get a little information about factors that are relevant to the problem (or coaching-related obstacle), from the coachee's perspective. This will help the coach when considering change-related interventions with the coachee in the session.

"What have you done to deal with the problem (or address the coaching-related obstacle)? If you have done something, what did you do that was helpful and what was not helpful?"

"What strengths and resiliency factors do you have as a person that you can use that might help you to deal with the problem (or address the coaching-related objective)?"

"Who in your life could support you as you deal with the problem (or address the coaching-related objective)?"

"Whom do you consider to be a role model who might directly or indirectly be helpful to you as you deal with your problem (or address the coaching-related objective)?"

"What core values do you have that we might refer to in our work together as you deal with the problem (or address the coaching-related objective)?"

"What principles do you have that guide your life that might be relevant to you as you deal with the problem (or address the coaching-related objective)?"

"How do you think I can best help you to deal with the problem (or address the coaching-related objective)?"

"Can you tell me about a problem that you dealt with effectively that was similar to the problem (or coaching-related obstacle) for which you are seeking coaching help now. How did you deal with the problem (or obstacle)?"

The purpose of this question is to help the coachee see that they may have already solved a similar problem or even the same problem in a different context and that they may be able to transfer their solution to the problem or coaching-related obstacle at hand. It is a core principle of SSC/OAATC that people actually have more skills and abilities than they think they have, and they have often lost sight of these skills/abilities. Helping to reacquaint them with these inner resources and encouraging them to see how they can use them to address their problem or coaching-related obstacle is an important task of SSC/OAATC coaches.

> "Between now and our face-to face-session, I would like to invite you to notice and note down anything that may indicate that things are changing for the better with respect to the problem (or coaching-related obstacle). Are you willing to do that?"

This is a version of Steve de Shazer's (1985) 'skeleton key' task. It is based on the idea that when someone has a problem, they tend to focus on that problem and not on signs that things may be changing for the better. If the coach has responded to the coachee's request for help, it is likely that the coachee is ready to address the problem and ready for change.

Other questions

> "What is your preferred way of learning is so that I can tailor the session to best help you?"

Coachees will vary in terms of how they best learn and it is useful for the coach to ask their coachee a question about their preferred learning style so that their learning preferences may be utilised when interventions are being planned in the session.

> "Is there anything that you would like me to know that will help me prepare for our face-to-face session or that will assist me in helping you get the most out of the session?

Rather than ask the coachee a number of questions about what might be important for the coach to know about them, it is better to invite the coachee themself to tell the coach about such information.

When the pre-session conversation is sufficient

While the purpose of the pre-session telephone conversation is to encourage both the coach and coachee to best prepare for the session, sometimes it transpires that this pre-session conversation is all the person needs to deal with the issue they have sought help for. The following are reasons why this may be the case.

Speaking about the issue enables the coachee to put it into a different perspective

This is mainly the case when the person is seeking help for a problem or coaching-related obstacle

Speaking about the issue helps the coachee to formulate a constructive course of action

Reviewing their strengths helps the coachee realise that they have the inner resources to address their problem (or coaching-related obstacle) or pursue their personal development on their own

Asking about the coachee's role model facilitates problem-based change or promotes development

Noticing change helps the coachee to see what is possible with respect to their problem (or coaching-related obstacle)

As a result, the coachee is able to see a way forward and wants to solve the problem or deal with the obstacle on their own. However, assuming that this is not the case after this conversation both the coach and coachee are prepared to meet for the session and to get the most out of it. Since SSC/OAATC coaches believe in the effective use of time, they tend to suggest scheduling the session soon after the pre-session contact but giving the coachee an opportunity to digest what they discussed over the phone and to prepare for the session itself.

Beginning the session

In this chapter, I will discuss a variety of issues to do with beginning the SSC/OAATC session.

Clarifying the purpose of the session and reiterating the nature of SSC/OAATC

At the very outset, whether or not the coach and coachee have had any pre-session contact other than to agree to have a single coaching session, it is vital that the coach and coachee reaffirm why they are having the session. This is to ensure that they are both on the same page concerning the session's purpose. Thus, the coach may say something like:

As we briefly discussed, Single-Session and One-At-A-Time coaching is concerned with helping you very quickly either set and pursue a personal development objective or identify and address an emotional problem or a coaching-related obstacle. This form of coaching builds on your strengths and helps you to use them in the service of what you want to get from the process. If you need it later, further coaching is available.

Then, the coach encourages the coachee to ask any questions about this opening statement before the coaching contract is formally agreed and possibly signed.

Before the session begins, it is likely that the coach and coachee have had some contact with one another. This contact may have been substantial, as when they have conversed on the telephone in preparation for the session (see Chapter 18), or it may have been less extensive as when the coach has asked the coachee to complete and return a pre-session form (see Table 17.1).

The coach begins by asking what the coachee learned from the pre-session contact and what they may have done since

Whether the coach and coachee had a pre-session telephone conversation or the coachee completed and returned a pre-session form, it is useful if the coach begins the session with some reference to a) this pre-session contact and what the coachee found beneficial from it and b) the work that the coachee may have done since this contact. Doing so helps to get the session off on a positive note and acknowledges the work that the coachee did both in the pre-session contact and subsequently. Here, the coach is acknowledging that the coachee has already initiated the change process and the role of the coach in the session helps them to capitalise on this. Here are a number of questions that an SSC/OAATC coach may ask at this point:

- "What did you find useful from our pre-session telephone conversation?"
- "With respect to what you want to get from this process, did you do anything since we spoke on the phone that has helped you in this regard? If so, what?"

In problem-focused SSC/OAATC, if the coach used the 'skeleton key' technique[1] suggested by de Shazer (1985), then it is important that they discover what change the coachee noticed:

- "What did you notice that may indicate that things are improving with respect to the problem (or coaching-related obstacle)?"

The coach can then use the coachee's response to further the discussion towards greater change.

The coach begins by referring to something that emerged from the pre-session contact

An alternative way of beginning the coaching session is where the coach refers to something that emerged from the pre-session contact. This again serves to provide a link between the pre-session contact and the session. Bearing in mind that the SSC/OAATC coach prefers the coachee to initiate the agenda rather than do so themself, it is rare for the coach to do this, but they will do so if the coachee struggles in this regard. For example, the coach may say something like:

I was struck by something you said when we spoke over the phone. You were talking about whether to pursue your personal development at work or with your relationships out of work, and then you mentioned your father, and I noticed your voice broke. How is your father related to your decision concerning what objective to pursue?

The coach begins the process when there has been no pre-session contact

When the coach and coachee have had no pre-session contact other than to set up an appointment for the session, then the coach begins the session by covering the following issues:

- As stressed at the beginning of the chapter, the coach should make sure that the coachee understands the nature of SSC/OAATC and should agree with them issues such as confidentiality, fees and how to access further coaching sessions, if needed
- The coach should ask the coachee what they hope to get from the session
- The coach could also ask the coachee how best they think the coach can help them

Covering these issues and asking the earlier questions are usually sufficient to initiate the session in SSC/OAATC.

Creating and keeping to a meaningful focus in the session

Perhaps the most critical skill that a coach needs to demonstrate in SSC/OAATC is the ability to create a meaningful focus with the coachee and once having done so, to remain with that focus. In discussing this issue, I note that there are general issues which apply to both development-focused SSC/OAATC and problem-focused SSC/OAATC and issues that are specific to each. The former issues are relevant to keeping to a focus once one has been created and the latter concerns more the creation of the focus. I will begin by considering the latter.

Creating a meaningful focus in development-focused SSC/OAATC

In development-focused SSC/OAATC, the coach's emphasis is on helping the coachee to develop themself meaningfully in one area of their life. Here is an example of how the coach can do this:

> *Coach:* In which one area of your life would you like to develop yourself
> *Coachee:* At work.
> *Coach:* In which one aspect of your work would you like to develop yourself?
> *Coachee:* Communication with other people at work.
> *Coach:* How would you like to develop yourself with respect to communicating with others at work?

Coachee: In the clarity of my communications
Coach: So, can we agree to focus on the clarity of your communications with others at work in the session?
Coachee: Yes.

In this segment, the coach helps the coachee to become more explicit about what they want to focus on during the session. Once a reasonable level of specificity has been expressed, the coach invites the coachee to make this the focus of the session.

Creating a meaningful focus in problem-focused SSC/OAATC

In problem-focused SSC/OAATC, the coach's emphasis is on helping the coachee either to address a problem that they have in life or to address a coaching-related obstacle if they are in ongoing development-focused coaching and their coach is not able to help them deal with this. Here is an example of how the coach can do this with a coachee whom I shall call 'Kate':

Coach: What problem (or coaching-related obstacle), would you like to address in the session?
Kate: I would like to address an anxiety problem.
Coach: Anxiety about what?
Kate: I am anxious about saying "no" to people at work.
Coach: So, can we agree to focus on the anxiety you feel when you have to say "no" to people at work?
Kate: Yes.

In this segment, the coach helps Kate to become more explicit about the problem that she wants to focus on during the session. Once a reasonable level of specificity has been expressed with respect to the problem, the coach invites the coachee to make this the focus of the session.

CREATING A MEANINGFUL FOCUS IN THE SESSION

Keeping to a focus once it has been agreed

Once the coach and coachee have agreed on a focus, it is important that both keep to this focus and it is largely the coach's responsibility to do this. There are a number of ways in which the coach can do this.

Bringing the coachee back to the agreed focus

It will often happen that even though the coach and coachee have agreed on a focus, then the coachee will sooner or later depart from this focus. Often this is nothing more than the natural human tendency to be reminded about something and to go off at a tangent when talking to another person. It is the same phenomenon as when one makes a shopping list but looks at other items not on one's list. Perhaps the most common and least invasive way in which the coach can help the coachee to keep to the agreed focus is to gently bring them back to that focus when they have moved away from it. The coach does this when they are clear that the departure is not relevant to the agreed focus.

Checking with the coachee that what is currently being discussed is relevant to the agreed focus

Sometimes the coach may not be sure if the coachee is departing from the agreed focus or not. In which case, it is useful to check this with the coachee. Thus, the coach may say something like, "Can I check something with you. I am not sure if your boss discussing the upcoming conference is relevant to your anxiety about saying 'no' to people. Can you help me with this?" Such an intervention either helps the coachee be clear about the topic's relevance or helps them see that it is not relevant and thus encourages them to return to the agreed focus.

Interrupting the coachee with tact

Occasionally, a coachee may go off at a tangent and may not respond to gentle and non-invasive attempts on the part of the coach to bring them back. In such cases, the coach needs to interrupt them. If it seems that the coachee will need to be interrupted, the best way I have found of doing so is to ask the coachee's permission to do so. I recommend saying something like, "Sometimes I may need to interrupt you to encourage us both to stay on track with our agreed focus. May I have your permission to do this?" In my experience, coachees are fine with this, often remarking that they know that they have the tendency to go off at a tangent and are grateful to be brought back. Once such permission has been given, it is easier for the coach to interrupt the coachee than when such permission has not been sought.

When the agreed focus turns out to be 'off'

One of the hallmarks of SSC/OAATC is that the coach checks periodically throughout the session that the agreed focus is still relevant. This should, ideally, obviate the possibility that the agreed focus is not the right one for the coachee. However, occasionally, the coach and coachee are well into the session when the coachee realises that their agreed focus is 'off' (meaning that it does not reflect the coachee's most pressing problem or most relevant area of personal development). If there is time, a new agreed focus should be worked with using as much of the material from the previous conversation as possible. However, if that is not possible, both coach and coachee may have to meet again to work with the correct focus.

Agreeing on a development-based process objective or problem-based process goal

At this point, the coach and coachee have agreed on a focus for the session. The next step is for them to agree where they are going with this focus. In development-focused coaching I call this a 'development-based objective', and in problem-focused coaching, I call this a 'problem-based goal'[1]. I will discuss these separately in this chapter.

Objectives in development-focused SSC/OAATC

It is important to distinguish between what may be called an 'outcome objective' and a 'process objective' in development-focused coaching. By an outcome objective, I mean what the coachee wants to achieve ultimately from development-focused coaching, while a process objective is a sign that there has been progress towards this outcome objective (in Chapter 7, I referred to this as a 'signpost'). While it is important for both coach and coachee to know what the coachee's outcome objective is, the primary purpose of SSC/OAATC is to help the coachee to set a process objective.

Features of a development-based outcome objective

I have previously outlined the main features of a good development-based outcome objective (Dryden, 2017a):

- It has a direction.
- It may have an endpoint, but it may also be ongoing.
- When it has an endpoint, this endpoint will have to be maintained.

- It tends to be broad, but with specific referents. Thus, if the coachee (whom I will call Liam) says that they want to be empathic at work (for example), the coach needs to help them to identify specific [S] markers of empathy that are measurable [M], achievable [A], relevant [R] to the coachee's nominated life domain and able to be achieved within a time [T] frame that is acceptable to the coachee (Dryden, 2017a).
- It has intrinsic rather than extrinsic importance.
- It is underpinned by values that are important to the coachee.
- It involves tasks that have intrinsic merit for the coachee.
- The coachee is able to integrate it into their life.
- The coachee is prepared to make sacrifices in order to achieve it.

As I said earlier, while it is important for the coach to agree on a development-based outcome objective with the coachee it is more important for the two of them to agree on a development-based process objective.

Agreeing on a development-based process objective

If the coach and coachee are aiming to have only one session, this process objective needs to be one that, if achieved, shows the coachee that they can work towards the outcome objective on their own. A suitable process objective is a clear benchmark of the outcome objective. In our example, it indicates to the coachee that they are on their way towards the outcome objective which is to be more empathic. It is important that by the end of the session the coachee thinks that they can achieve the process objective and thus be able to achieve the outcome objective on their own. Here is an example:

Coach: So, you would like to be more empathic at work?
Liam: Yes
Coach: How would you know when you have achieved your objective?
Liam: I would communicate my understanding of the other person's perspective every time I have a conversation with someone at work that calls for such understanding.

Coach: What would tell you that you were on your way to achieving your objective?
Liam: If I would show understanding half the time I have a conversation with people at work that calls for such understanding.
Coach: If you achieved that do you think that you could travel the rest of the way on your own?
Liam: Yes, I think so.
Coach: So let's see if by working together you think by the end of the session that you can get to that half-way stage. OK?
Liam: That would be good.

If the coach and coachee have agreed a 'one session at a time' contract, the process objective can be one that gives the coachee something to work towards before having another coaching session. Then, at that further session, another process objective is set. The coach and coachee in development-focused OAATC will work one session at a time until, at some point, the coachee will decide that they can journey the rest of the way on their own and that this will mark their final session.

Goals in problem-focused SSC/OAATC

When a person comes to coaching looking for help with a problem or is stuck in their ongoing coaching with another coach because they have encountered an obstacle[2], then the coach will practise problem-focused coaching within a single-session, one-at-a-time context. In this kind of work, SSC/OAATC coaches tend to fall into camps: those that prefer to work only with solutions[3] or those that work with both problems and solutions.

Understanding the problem or coaching-related obstacle

In this section, I will distinguish between 'stated' problems and 'assessed' problems.

'Stated' problems. Often it is clear what the coachee's *stated* problem is since they have revealed it when agreeing on a focus with their coach.

Let me use the example of Kate who revealed (in Chapter 20) that her problem was anxiety about saying "no" to people at work. Now if we just take Kate's *stated* problem here, then it is possible for her coach to ask her what she wants to achieve with respect to this problem. I call this the 'goal with respect to the *stated* problem'. If the coach asked Kate for her goal at this point, it is likely that she would have said, "to say 'no' to people at work when I want to do so". On the face of it, this is fine. However, as the coach does not know what is anxiety-provoking about saying "no" for Kate, it is probable that she would struggle to achieve her 'goal with respect to the stated problem' since she would still be anxious when she came to say "no". Thus, the coach needs to do some assessment of this problem so that they can help Kate deal with her anxiety.

'Assessed' problems. Let's suppose that Kate is most anxious about being disliked by the other person when she has said "no" to them. This is then her *assessed* problem since it involves both her *feelings* (in this case 'anxiety') and the *adversity* she feels most anxious about (in this case 'being disliked'). The goal that is revealed after such an assessment has been done is what I call the 'goal with respect to the *assessed* problem'. Once the assessed problem has been revealed, the coach can ask Kate questions such as:

- "If you were to say 'no' to a person and they were to dislike you, what would be a constructive way of dealing with their dislike?"

If Kate were to achieve this goal (with respect to the *assessed* problem) then she would have dealt with her anxiety, and she would be able to achieve her goal (with respect to her *stated* problem) of saying "no" to people at work.

In short, a goal with respect to a stated problem may not necessarily help a coachee deal with the adversity that is often at the heart of the problem, whereas a goal with respect to an assessed problem will help them to do this. Consequently, I advise coaches whom

I supervise to carry out an assessment of their coachees' problems before setting problem-based goals with them.

Emotional goals and behavioural goals in problem-focused SSC/OAATC

When formulating a problem-based goal with the coachee, the coach needs to keep the adversity (that is a central part of the problem) to the fore. Then, the goal needs to include an emotional response to the adversity (the 'emotional goal') and a behavioural response to the adversity (the 'behavioural goal'). But first, the coach needs to discover the coachee's problematic emotional and behavioural responses to the adversity, and this should be done as part of the problem assessment. Thus, in the case of Kate, the coach needs to discover her problematic emotional and behavioural responses to the problem-related adversity (i.e. being disliked for saying "no"). In this case, it is clear what these responses are. She feels *anxious* about the prospect of being disliked, and she *avoids facing* this prospect by not saying "no". Once the coach knows the coachee's problematic emotional and behavioural responses to the adversity, then they can help the person set healthy emotional and behavioural responses to this adversity as goals. Here is how Kate's coach helped her to do this:

> *Coach:* So, you feel anxious about being disliked, and you avoid it by not saying "no" when you want to do so. Is that correct?
> *Kate:* Yes.
> *Coach:* So, in order for you to be able to say "no" I need to help you deal more constructively with the prospect of being disliked. Does that make sense?
> *Kate:* Yes it does.
> *Coach:* Now, instead of anxiety, what would be a healthy emotional response to being disliked?
> *Kate:* To be unconcerned about it?
> *Coach:* Well, the problem with that is that since being disliked is an adversity, it is healthy to feel negative about it rather than feel

nothing. Now, anxiety is a negative emotion that is unhealthy, so we are looking for a negative emotion that is healthy.

Kate: So, to be concerned about it?

Coach: Yes, un-anxiously concerned. Does that make sense?

Kate: Yes, it does.

Coach: Now, what would be a healthy alternative to avoiding being disliked?

Kate: Facing it.

Coach: So, would you like me to help you to face up to being disliked and to be concerned, but not anxious about facing it?

Kate: Yes, that seems a good goal.

Coach: And would that help you to say "no" to people at work when you want to do so?

Kate: Yes, it would.

What this interchange shows is that it is healthy to feel a negative emotion in response to a negative event as long as this emotion is linked to behaviour that helps the coachee to face and deal with the adversity in question.

Outcome goals and process goals in problem-focused SSC/OAATC

As with development-focused SSC/OAATC, in problem-focused SSC/OAATC, it is also important to distinguish between an 'outcome goal' and a 'process goal'. As before, an outcome goal is what the coachee wants to achieve ultimately from problem-focused coaching, and a process goal is a sign that there has been progress towards this outcome goal. Again, while it is important for both coach and coachee to know what the coachee's outcome goal is, the primary purpose of SSC/OAATC is to help the coachee to set a process goal.

In the case of Kate, this means that the coach needs to help her to specify a process goal which indicates to her that she is making progress towards her outcome goal and that she can work towards the outcome goal independently.

Identifying and utilising important coaching variables in the session

In Chapter 18, I discussed how the coach and coachee could prepare for the session by having a pre-session telephone conversation. During this conversation, the coach helps the coachee to identify a number of variables that may help them during the session. It is important for the coach to keep a list of these factors and keep them in mind during the session. Doing so is important since an opportunity may present itself for the coach to suggest to the coachee that they may use one of these factors to either enhance their development or address their problem (or coaching-related obstacle). Here is a list of such variables.

Internal strengths and resiliency factors

Here the coach may suggest to the coachee that they can use a particular strength or resiliency factor on the path towards their development-based objective or while addressing their problem. For example, Kate's coach could suggest that she use her persistence (one of her nominated strengths) to address her fear of being disliked since it is likely that she will only deal with this problem effectively once she has faced the possibility of being disliked many times.

Values

Encouraging the coachee to act in ways that are consistent with a core value is particularly useful in both development-focused SSC/

OAATC and problem-focused SSC/OAATC. Kate listed 'honesty' as one of her core values and her coach encouraged her to think of his value when deciding whether or not to say "no" to a person at work. The concept of values has a central role in 'Acceptance and Commitment Coaching' (Hill & Oliver, 2019).

Previous attempts to solve the problem

In problem-focused SSC/OAATC, it is particularly important for the coach to discover what the coachee has previously tried to deal with the problem. In doing so, the coach encourages the coachee to capitalise on anything that was helpful and to avoid using strategies that were unhelpful. Previously, Kate tried to deal with her problem by avoiding it, and she saw in the session that this only served to maintain her problem. She resolved to 'avoid her avoidance' and to seek out situations at work where it was possible that she may be disliked by saying "no".

Successful attempts to deal with similar problems

It is useful to ask the coachee whether they have been successful at solving similar problems to the one for which they are currently seeking help. This often reveals helpful strategies that the coachee can transfer to the current problem.

Helping others

Similarly, it is useful to ask the coachee how they would help someone who sought their assistance in dealing with being disliked as a prelude to saying "no" to others at work. Once the coach has encouraged the coachee to identify the helpful ingredients in the assistance that they would offer the other person, the coach explores with the coachee whether or not they would be willing to follow their own counsel and if not, why not.

> *Coach:* If a friend came to you for advice on how to deal with being disliked by a work colleague at work whom she said "no" to, how would you suggest they handle such dislike?
> *Kate:* I would say to them that it is unpleasant to be disliked, but it's more important to be honest in one's dealings with work colleagues. I would also remind my friend that while some people may dislike her for saying "no", others will respect her for doing so and at work, it's more important to be respected than liked.
> *Coach:* Is it possible that you can apply this viewpoint to yourself?
> *Kate:* I was thinking the very same thing!

Being helped by others

Asking the coachee how they have been or could be helped by others can also be useful in helping them to address their current problem. The coach can do with respect to the problem at hand or in general.

Applied to the current problem

Here, the coach could ask Kate:
- "Have others been helpful to you at all when you told them about your anxiety about being disliked?"
- "If you told someone in your life whom you generally find helpful about this problem, what could they say that you would find constructive?"

The coach can use these responses to assist the coachee themself or as a suggestion of how the coachee can help themself.

In general

Here the coach could ask Kate:

- "Whom do you find helpful in your life? What do they do or say to you that you find constructive?"

Again, the coach can use the coachee's response as a way of helping the coachee themself or as a suggestion of how the coachee can help themself.

Role models

Referring to a role model can be particularly useful to a coachee when they address their problem in problem-focused SST/OAATC. In my experience, good role models are seen as struggling to deal with a problem but address it effectively in the end. While holding a salient role model and an associated self-helping message in mind, it is useful if the coachee could have to hand a photo of the person or a relevant memento that serves as a reminder of the person.

Guiding principles

A guiding principle is a helpful saying or maxim that helps to guide the person in an important area of their life (see Chapter 18). One of Kate's guiding principles that was useful to her as she addressed her anxiety of being disliked related to saying "no" to colleagues at work was "Honesty is the best policy". This reflected the core value of honesty that she also referred to in the session.

External resources

External resources refer to anything or anybody in the coachee's environment that can aid the coaching process. It can include:

- Organisations that offer specialist help related to the coachee's problem, for example, or that can aid the pursuit of their development-based objective.
- Phone apps that help the coachee monitor their behaviour or practice an important skill.
- People in the coachee's life who might support the person as they pursue their development-based objective or address their problem.

Kate nominated members of her book group as those who could support her as she addressed her anxiety of being disliked. The theme of the book group was particularly apposite as the books they read and discussed were those that dealt with psychological self-help.

Facilitating change in SSC/OAATC: General factors

Coaching involves change. In development-focused coaching, the coachee normally has to give up something to focus on their personal development, and they may have to change various things to maximise the chances that they will achieve their development-based objective. In problem-focused coaching, if the problem is going to be effectively addressed, then the coachee needs to change the factors that are responsible for the existence of the problem if these can be changed or develop a healthy attitude towards these factors if they can't be changed.

In this chapter, I will discuss some important *general* change-relevant factors that are relevant to promote in both development-focused SSC/OAATC and problem-focused SSC/OAATC. In the following two chapters I will discuss change factors that are more specific to each one respectively.

There are many factors that promote change in both forms of SSC/OAATC and no doubt different coaches would emphasise different factors. So what follows is a personal approach to this topic. Thus, I have found the following factors to be particularly constructive in my practice of both forms of SSC/OAATC.

Expectation, intention and realism

If both coach and coachee approach the single session expecting that something meaningful can come out of it for the coachee and they do so with the intention of making that happen then these are essential ingredients for change in SSC/OAATC. However, these mindsets need to be tempered by realism, and it is the coach's task to help the coachee develop a realistic view of what they can get from the situation and what they probably can't get from it.

Realism in development-focused SSC/OAATC

Thus, in development-focused SSC, the coach can help the coachee to a) identify an area of their life in which they can develop themself and what an achievable objective might be in this life area; b) develop an action plan to work towards this objective and how to implement it; and c) identify and have a plan to deal with possible obstacles along the way. Helping the person take the first steps may be all that is needed, and if not, they may benefit more from development-focused OAATC where the tasks are the same, but the coach and coachee meet for one session at a time to do this work. This is why it is important in SSC, in particular, for the coach to make clear that while they may get the work done in one session, more sessions are possible.

Realism in problem-focused SSC/OAATC

In problem-focused SSC, the coach can help the coachee to a) identify and focus on the problem[1] for which the person is seeking help and develop a problem-related goal; b) understand the factors that maintain the problem[2]; c) identify ways of dealing with these factors[3] and develop a possible solution to the problem; d) rehearse the solution in the session; e) develop an action plan to practise the solution and how to implement it and f) identify and have a plan to deal with possible obstacles along the way. Again, helping the person take the first steps along this path may be sufficient, but if not, problem-focused OAATC can help to deal with these tasks one session at a time.

SSC/OAATC is particularly suited for people who are stuck with a problem and want to take the first steps to become unstuck or who would like help to get started to develop themselves but want to take over the reins as soon as possible. If the coachee has unrealistic expectations of the process, then it is important for the coach to focus on these and help them to see what can and cannot realistically be gained from SSC/OAATC.

Acceptance[4]

Acceptance is a 'buzzword' in coaching and therapy at the moment, and when the coach uses the term, it is important for them to clarify what they mean by it. It is particularly useful in problem-focused SSC/OAATC when related to an adversity, and when I use it in this context, I mean the following. The person:

- Acknowledges that an adversity exists and what its nature is.
- Evaluates the adversity negatively.
- Prefers that the adversity does not exist, does not demand that this is the case and recognises that conditions are in place which explains its existence.
- Attempts to change the adversity and relevant conditions if they can be changed and constructively adjusts and gets on with other aspects of life if they can't be changed.

It is clear from this definition that acceptance does not mean 'passive resignation', or 'complacency', but, as the last point shows, it can be a prelude to the person changing what can be changed and constructively adjusting to what can't be changed.

Discomfort tolerance

Change is uncomfortable, especially if it is meaningful, so it is vital for the coach to help the coachee to develop a 'discomfort tolerance' mindset. There are two types of discomfort that it is important for coaches to tolerate if they are to get the most from

SSC/OAATC. The first type of discomfort tends to be acute, and it is the type of discomfort that comes with distressing emotions such as anxiety. Here, the coachee responds by avoiding the situations in which they would otherwise feel acutely uncomfortable. This type of discomfort is more often found in problem-focused SSC/OAATC since such problems often involve the experience of distressing emotions in the face of adversities. The second type of discomfort is more 'low-level' than the first type. It involves the person going from comfort to discomfort before later becoming comfortable as they engage in tasks that are beneficial for them in the longer term. This is the kind of discomfort associated with non-anxiety-based procrastination and when in this state people often say that they are not 'in the mood' to do what is in their best interests to do. This type of discomfort is found in both types of SSC/OAATC. When found in development-focused SSC/OAATC it often explains why the coachee does not follow through on implementing their action plan. When found in problem-focused SSC/OAATC, it often explains why the coachee does not implement their solution in real-life solutions.

The components of discomfort tolerance

Discomfort tolerance involves the coachee developing a mindset which compromises the following components:

1. Recognising that it is a struggle to deal with discomfort.
2. Acknowledging that it is possible to tolerate discomfort.
3. Showing oneself that it is in one's healthy interests to tolerate discomfort (when it is).
4. Determining that one will take steps to tolerate discomfort
5. Taking those steps.
6. Repeating 1–5 whenever necessary.

Given the ubiquitous nature of the 'discomfort intolerance' mindset, I recommend that coaches raise this issue with coachees as a possible roadblock to progress in both forms of coaching discussed in this book.

Action

When the coachee comes away from a single session of coaching with a good idea but without the determination to act on that idea, then they won't get as much from the session as they could have. I call this phenomenon 'cognition without ignition' (Dryden, 1985a).

Action in development-focused SSC/OAATC

Taking action is usually the key to pursuing and achieving the coachee's objective in development-focused SSC/OAATC and involves them implementing their action plan (see Chapter 24). As such, action in development-focused SSC/OAATC can be seen to fall into one of three categories:

- Category 1: Action that is in the service of the coachee's objective.
- Category 2: Action that goes against the coachee's objective.
- Category 3: Action that is not relevant to the coachee's objective.

As such, roadblocks in development-focused coaching occur when the coachee spends insufficient time in category 1 along with too much time in category 3 and when the coachee spends any time in category 2. The coach should explore these with the coachee as possible roadblocks so that some planning can be done to either avoid them from occurring or deal with them if they occur (see Chapter 28).

Action in problem-focused SSC/OAATC

Taking action is also central to change occurring in problem-focused SSC/OAATC and in helping the coachee to reach their problem-related goal. Such action usually involves the coachee facing the adversity that is a key part of their problem but doing so in a sensible way. I have termed this sensible way, 'challenging, but not overwhelming', a phrase which I use with coachees particularly in problem-focused coaching (Dryden, 1985b). This describes the situation where the coachee undertakes to face the relevant adversity, armed with constructive ways of dealing with it that is a challenge for them but not overwhelming to them at that given time. The coachee determines this for themself experientially. The more the coachee faces the adversity, the less they consider situations that feature the adversity to be overwhelming.

Action in problem-focused SSC/OAATC can be seen to fall into one of the following categories:

- Category 1: Action that is in the service of the coachee's problem-related goal.
- Category 2: Action that perpetuates the coachee's problem and thus goes against their goal.
- Category 3: Action that is not relevant to the coachee's problem or goal.

Similar to roadblocks in development-focused coaching, roadblocks in problem-focused coaching occur when the coachee spends insufficient time in category 1 along with too much time in category 3 and when the coachee spends any time in category 2. It is important for the coach to discourage the coachee from using strategies that aim to give them a sense of comfort and safety while facing the adversity. These are known as safety-seeking manoeuvres. In using them, the coachee unwittingly perpetuates their problem in the longer term, and thus the coach should be encouraged to tolerate discomfort rather than aim to feel comfortable and safe while facing adversity.

The coach should discuss these roadblocks with the coachee to determine which may occur as the coachee sets out to deal with their problem. Doing so helps the coachee plan to either prevent them from occurring or deal with them if they occur (again see Chapter 28).

Value-based action

While I have discussed action that is the service of the coachee's objective/goal, I also want to mention action that is in service of the coachee's values as a coachee is more likely to take action when such action is in the service of both their objective/goal and a core value

(Hill & Oliver, 2019). This is relevant to both development-focused SSC/OAATC and problem-focused SSC/OAATC. Thus, when Kate reminded herself of her core value of 'honesty', this helped her to say "no" to her work colleagues when it was in her interests to do so.

Having discussed some *general* change-related factors in this chapter, in the next two chapters, I will discuss such factors that are *specific* to each form of SSC/OAATC respectively.

Facilitating change in development-focused SSC/OAATC

In the previous chapter, I discussed important general change factors in SSC/OAATC. In this chapter, I will focus on specific change factors related to development-focused SSC/OAATC and in the following chapter, I will focus on the same issue with respect to problem-focused SSC/OAATC.

Facilitating change in development-focused SSC/OAATC involves helping the coachee to do one or more of the following:

- Change their mindset
- Change some aspect of their environment
- Change their behaviour

Helping the coachee to change their mindset

Once the coach has helped the coachee set a development-based objective, it is useful for the coach to ensure that the coachee has a mindset that maximises their chance or reaching their objective. Anything that prevents a coach from being fully committed to their objective should be a target for change. In this section, I will focus on mindset factors that need to be the target for change. The coach can do this in a number of ways. First, the coach can ask the coachee questions concerning why they have selected this particular objective at this particular time. Second, they can ask the coachee if they had set the objective before and stopped pursuing it. The coachee's responses to such questions sometimes reveal a mindset that is less than optimal and this mindset should be a target for change if the coachee's path to the objective is to be as smooth as possible.

Here is an example of how a coach worked with Liam (whom we met in Chapter 21) on this point and helped Liam to change his mindset. If you recall, Liam's development-based objective was to become more empathic at work.

> *Coach:* So, have you tried to be more empathic at work before or is this the first time you have set this objective?
>
> *Liam:* Yes, I have tried before as part of the coaching I had before.
>
> *Coach:* So, what happened?
>
> *Liam:* Well, it was suggested that I focus on this as part of a previous appraisal and I wasn't convinced.
>
> *Coach:* So, you kind of went along with it, but it didn't really come from you. Is that it?
>
> *Liam:* Well, it came from me about 25%
>
> *Coach:* What is that percentage now?
>
> *Liam:* More like 75%
>
> *[While Liam is now more signed up to the objective of being more empathic at work than previously, there is still a doubt in his mind which may represent some specific factor that needs to be changed if Liam is going to be fully signed up to his objective. As the coach would like Liam to be fully committed to his objective, she proceeds as follows.]*
>
> *Coach:* So, what would it take for you to be fully committed to your objective?
>
> *Liam:* Good question. Well, I would be fully committed if I decided for myself without me being told to do it.
>
> *Coach:* So, let me see if I understand. If it was left to you, you would be 100% committed to becoming more empathic at work, but that percentage comes down to 75% when somebody tells you to do it. Is that right?
>
> *Liam:* Yes, autonomy is very important to me.
>
> *Coach:* I can hear that, although you and I seem to have a different view of autonomy.

Liam: Really? What do you mean?

Coach: Well, from what you have said, you see autonomy as having the freedom to do something that is important to you without any interference from others. Right?

Liam: Right.

Coach: I see autonomy as having the freedom to do something that is important even though someone else wants you to do it.

Liam: Oh, I see. So, I'm not as free as I think I am because it will only take someone telling me to do something I already want to do to spoil it for me a bit.

Coach: So, it only takes your boss to tell you to work on becoming more empathic to affect your motivation. If you were genuinely autonomous, you could be 100% committed to your objective whether your boss told you to do it or not.

Liam: I really like that. I can be free to do what I want whether somebody tells me to do it or not. That is really going to make a big difference to me.

[What the coach has done is to question Liam's mindset concerning autonomy. Helping Liam to rethink his views on the subject led to a significant change which allowed the coachee to become fully committed to his objective.]

Helping the coachee to change their environment

Sometimes it is vital for the coachee to change their environment if they are to give themself the best chance to help themself achieve their development-based objective. One way in which environmental change is important concerns the time the coach will need to devote to pursuing their objective. In some cases, this means that the coachee gives up an activity, for example, and devotes the time saved to pursuing their objective. The coach needs to discuss with the coachee how they feel about giving up the activity and whether or not they are prepared to do so. The coach needs to help the coachee understand that change involves making sacrifices and although they may not like this fact, they can make the change without liking it. Helping the coachee to keep in mind why they have chosen to pursue the objective and any values that underpin it are useful strategies in this respect.

Making simple environmental changes while the coachee is pursuing their development-based objective can sometimes be surprisingly powerful. Thus, Liam's coach suggested that Liam might think of taking a work colleague away from their workspace to try and understand their point of view about a relevant topic. Hitherto, Liam had tried to understand his colleague's point of view in his office which was intimidating for the colleague and awkward for Liam. This simple change in environment proved to be very useful in helping Liam to achieve his objective.

Helping the coachee to change their behaviour

In development-focused coaching, the coachee will need to take action if they are to achieve their development-based objective. It is useful for the coach to explore with the coachee what the person plans to do to achieve their objective. Sometimes it will be clear to the coach that the behaviour that the person plans to implement is not likely to be effective in helping them to achieve their objective in which case the coach needs to 'level' with the coachee and explain clearly their concerns on this issue. Then the coach needs to get feedback from the coachee before initiating a dialogue on behavioural alternatives.

Sometimes it is clear that the coachee lacks the skills that are needed to achieve their development objective. In which case, the SSC/OAATC coach needs to form an opinion whether they can teach these skills in the single session or whether it would be best to encourage the coachee to learn those skills elsewhere and then return when they have done so. This latter scenario is consistent with Single-Session Coaching and particularly with One-At-A-Time Coaching. For example, if it transpired that Liam lacked the skills to communicate empathically and could not be taught them in the session, then he would be encouraged to access empathy training and return for another coaching session when he has done that.

Facilitating change in problem-focused SSC/OAATC

In dealing with the coachee's problem (or coaching-related obstacle) in SSC/OAATC, the coach needs to be focused on the coachee's process goal[1] in deciding with the person what needs to be changed. In discussing this topic, I will use the example of Kate who we first met in Chapter 20. If you recall, Kate's *stated* problem was anxiety about saying "no" to colleagues at work, and her goal with respect to this *stated* problem was to be able to say "no" to them. When the coach assessed Kate's problem it emerged that her *assessed* problem was anxiety about being disliked by her colleagues should she say "no" to them which led her not to assert herself. Her goal with respect to her *assessed* problem was to be concerned, but not anxious about being disliked. In this chapter, I will focus on facilitating change with respect to problem-focused SSC/OAATC.

Change the factors that maintain the problem: the example of Kate

In problem-focused coaching, the emphasis is on understanding how the person unwittingly maintains the problem rather than how it originated. In Kate's case she maintained her problem by a number of factors:

- By thinking that her work colleagues will dislike her if she says "no" to them.
- By overemphasising the importance of being liked at work rather than being respected.

- By the attitude that she took to being disliked.
- By avoiding dealing with the issue by saying "yes" to her work colleagues when it would be in her best interests to say "no".

When the coach and coachee have identified such factors, the coach asks the coachee which of these factors have to be changed to enable the coachee to achieve their problem-related goals with respect to both their *stated* and *assessed* problems. In Kate's case, she argued that the last *three* were important especially her attitude to being disliked.

1. As we saw in Chapter 22, Kate came to see that being respected was more important than being liked in a work context since her work colleagues are not her friends.
2. The coach helped Kate to see the importance of facing the adversity of being disliked.
3. Kate thought that she needed to develop a more resilient attitude towards being disliked in order to face this adversity. I will illustrate how Kate's coach helped her address her attitude later in the chapter.

Helping the coachee to face the adversity and deal with it

In my view, it is important for the coachee to stop avoiding the adversity which is at the heart of their problem and start facing it. As I discussed in Chapter 23, this is best done by the principle known as 'challenging, but not overwhelming' where the coach faces a challenging example of their adversity rather than one that is overwhelming for them (Dryden, 1985b). In order to do this, the coach needs to help the coachee to take a stance towards the adversity. The main purpose of such a stance is to help the coach to face the adversity without the use of safety-seeking strategies so that they can process the adversity properly.

Encouraging the coachee to adopt a healthy stance towards the adversity

There are a number of stances that a coach can encourage the coachee to take towards an adversity and I will review them here.

Helping the coachee to develop a healthy attitude towards an adversity

Encouraging a coachee to develop a healthy attitude towards adversity in problem-focused SSC/OAATC is perhaps the most challenging stance to help a coachee to adopt. This involves initially encouraging the coachee to assume temporarily that the adversity is what they think it is. Thus, in Kate's case, her adversity was 'being disliked'. Recall that she did not say "no" to work colleagues for fear that they would dislike her. Now, this is an inference which in Kate's case is a prediction of what would happen if she acted in a certain way. It can be put into an 'if...then' form. Namely, "If I say 'no' to my colleagues, then they will dislike me". This may be correct or incorrect. If we take the position that Kate is anxious about being disliked because she holds an anxiety-based attitude towards this adversity, she will not develop a healthy attitude towards it by assuming that the adversity will not happen. She needs to assume temporarily that she will be disliked and consider what attitude she can take towards that which will be healthy for her and lead to her goal which, as we saw in Chapter 21, was to be concerned about being disliked, but not anxious about it.

It transpired that Kate's anxiety-based attitude towards being disliked was as follows: 'If I am disliked then there is something wrong with me'. This is how her SSC/OAATC coach helped her to reflect on and change this attitude:

Coach: So, you think that if someone dislikes you, then there is something wrong with you?
Kate: Yes, I do.

Coach: When you operate on that attitude, do you mean that there may be something wrong with an aspect of you, but not through and through or do you mean that there is something wrong with you through and through?

[The coach asks this question to clarify what Kate's attitude means since it is not clear what it means on the surface.]

Kate: I mean that I feel as if I am defective.

Coach: And that feeling proves what?

Kate: That I am defective.

Coach: When you stand back and think about it, what do you think about this attitude?

Kate: It doesn't seem very healthy.

Coach: Do you think it's true?

Kate: Yes, I do, unfortunately.

Coach: If a good friend came to you and said that if someone dislikes her, it proves that there is something wrong with her, what would you say to her?

Kate: I would say that that is not true.

Coach: So, you would not say, "I agree with you there is something wrong with you and that you are defective"?

Kate: No, of course not.

Coach: Why not?

Kate: Because she isn't defective.

Coach: But doesn't her being disliked make her defective?

Kate: No.

Coach: Why not?

Kate: Because if someone doesn't like her, it may say something more about the other person or my friend may have done something dislikeable, but neither of these reasons is proof that she is defective.

Coach: So, if she is not defective in this case what is she?

Kate: An ordinary human being....I see what you are getting at.

Coach: What's that?

Kate: You are encouraging me to view myself as I would view my friend.

Coach: That's right. Would you like to be able to do so?

Kate: Definitely.
Coach: You can.
Kate: How?
Coach: First, by questioning your old attitude and comparing with the new attitude; second, by imagining yourself being disliked and holding the new attitude and third, by acting on that new attitude while saying "no" to work colleagues.

Helping the coachee to place the adversity in a different frame ('reframing')

Helping the coachee to develop a healthy attitude towards an adversity, as we have seen, involves the SSC/OAATC coach encouraging the coachee to focus on that adversity (in Kate's case, 'being disliked'). The spotlight is on the adversity and the adversity alone. When the coach helps the coachee to reframe the adversity, they help the coachee to consider the adversity in a new frame which includes all relevant variables and not just the adversity. In doing so, the coach helps the coachee to reflect on the place of the adversity within the new frame. Thus, if the coach asked Kate what is more important to her, to be liked by her work colleagues or to be respected by them, then what the coach is doing is introducing 'respect' into the frame. If Kate responds by saying that being respected at work is more important than being liked, then a reframe has taken place. Now the coach can help Kate to see that if she says "no" to people at work, she still might be disliked, but she will probably be respected, and as she has prioritised respect over being liked, this reframing of the adversity of being disliked will help her to achieve her goal of saying "no".

Questioning the coachee's inference/adversity

As pointed out earlier in this chapter, an adversity is basically an inference about what happened or what may happen in a given situation. Thus, when Kate predicts that if she says "no" to a work colleague, then that person will dislike her, she is making an inference and thus this inference, for all intents and purposes, is her adversity.

In the attitude change stance discussed earlier, the coach encourages the coachee to assume that their inference/adversity is correct with the purpose of encouraging the person to change their attitude towards the adversity.

When using reframing, the coach also works with the coachee on the assumption that the inference/adversity is correct but helps the person put the adversity in a more constructive frame.

When the SSC/OAATC coach helps the coachee to stand back and question the inference, they ask questions concerning the validity of the inference and whether or not there is a more likely explanation of what happened. Adopting this stance with Kate, her coach would ask her questions such as:

- "What is the likelihood that your work colleagues will dislike you if you say 'no' to them?"
- "Would you dislike a work colleague if they said 'no' to you? If not, how do you know that your colleagues would dislike you for saying 'no' to them?"

The purpose of inference questioning is to help the coachee develop a more likely, more benign inference of the available data.

Changing the adversity

If the SSC/OAATC coach cannot help the coachee change their attitude towards an adversity, put it into a healthier frame or develop a more benign inference, then they may encourage the person to change the adversity, if it can be changed, or leave it if it can't be changed. In my view, while this is the least satisfactory of the four stances discussed in this chapter, sometimes it is the best one, mainly if the adversity is particularly aversive.

Before leaving this issue, I want to make two points. First, the stances discussed in the chapter are not mutually exclusive and second, the coachee is the best person to select the stance that is best for them.

Action planning and implementation in development-focused SSC/OAATC

In this chapter, I will discuss how the coach works with the coachee to help them to develop an action plan and talk about how they can implement it. An action plan is just that – a plan of actions that the coachee needs to enact to achieve their development-based objective.

Helping the coachee to devise an action plan

When the coach helps the coachee to devise an action plan with respect to their developmental-based objective, the following steps should be considered:

Helping the coachee to set clear benchmarks for monitoring progress towards their development-based objective

In Chapter 21, I made the point that while the coachee's development-based objective may be broad (e.g. "I want to be empathic at work"), it is important that it also has specific referents. These specific markers can be made clear by the coachee in ways so that they serve as benchmarks of progress towards their objective.

Helping the coachee to map out a realistic timeline for achieving the objective

It is useful for the coachee to give themself sufficient time to go from benchmark to benchmark in working to achieve their development-focused objective given their other life responsibilities and the coach should help them to plan this.

Helping the coachee to list the actions that they need to take to achieve the objective

Once the timeline has been established, the coach should help the coachee to specify actions they need to take to meet it.

Encouraging the coachee to use their strengths and other helping resources

When helping the coachee devise an action plan, the coach should encourage them to use their strengths and other resources that the coach helped them to identify earlier.

Helping the coachee to integrate the action plan into their life

The coachee needs to integrate the action plan into their life to maximise the chances that they will implement it. If there is any doubt about this, then the coach needs to encourage the coachee either to modify their schedule so that they can implement their plan or to modify the plan so that they can incorporate it into their life and thus implement it.

Helping the coachee to implement the action plan

In ongoing coaching, the coach has time to help the coachee to do a number of things including: i) developing a way of monitoring the implementation of the action plan; ii) understanding and dealing with actual obstacles to coachee progress; iii) capitalising on success and iv) maintaining their gains once they have met their objective. If the coach and coachee have an OAATC contract where they agree to meet one session at a time, then the coach may be able to help the coachee in the previously mentioned ways (see Dryden, 2018c). However, since at the outset the coach and coachee do not know how much contact they are going to have, the best that the coach can do is to help the coachee to identify in advance and have a plan to deal with possible roadblocks to the implementation of the action plan. This is the subject of Chapter 28.

Rehearsing, action planning and implementing the solution in problem-focused SSC/OAATC

In problem-focused SSC/OAATC, the coach works with the coachee to develop a potential solution to the problem for which the coachee has sought help. If the coach adopts both a problem- and solution-focused approach to SSC/OAATC, this solution is based on an accurate assessment of the problem and deals adequately with the major factors that explain the existence of the problem and why the person has not been able to deal with it. The solution also needs to be able to help the coachee to achieve their problem-related goal. However, if the coach adopts a solution-focused approach to SSC/OAATC then as the name makes clear the emphasis is on developing a solution that helps coachee to reach their goal. In this chapter, I discuss how coach and coachee agree a solution in problem-focused SSC/OAATC and how they together choose potential solutions.

The process of the coach and coachee agreeing a solution in problem-focused SSC/OAATC involves both people discussing potential solutions and selecting one that best meets the following criteria:

- The solution should be able to solve the problem if implemented properly.
- The coachee should be able to integrate the solution into their life or make a change to thus integrate it.
- The coachee should have skills to put the solution into practice.
- The solution should ideally have no 'side-effects'. Thus, it should not create a new problem while solving the problem for which the coachee has sought help. Sometimes this cannot be

avoided, and when this is the case, the coachee should anticipate this and be prepared to 'exchange' the new problem for the old, as it were.
- The coachee should be prepared to implement the solution until the problem has been solved.

Types of solution

Let me review the main types of solution that a coachee can implement. These include:

A behavioural solution

Here, the coachee puts into practice a solution that involves a change in behaviour (e.g. assertion).

A cognitive solution

Here, the coachee changes their attitude towards the adversity, reframes it or changes their inference (see Chapter 25). This may involve acceptance of an adversity that cannot be changed.

A cognitive-behavioural solution

Here, the coachee puts into practice a solution that involves both a change in behaviour and an associated change in thinking.

An environmental solution

Here, the coachee solves their problem by changing a relevant aspect of their environment which is centrally implicated in their problem.

Rehearsing the solution in the session

Once the solution has been agreed between coach and coachee, the next step is for the coach to encourage the coachee to rehearse the solution in the session.

Why the coachee should rehearse the solution in the session

Elsewhere I argued that rehearsing the solution in the session enables the coachee to answer the following questions (Dryden, 2019d):

Does the solution feel right to me? A solution may seem the best on offer in theory, but only if the coachee takes it out for a 'test run' will they get an experiential sense that it is right.

Can I make the solution work? Rehearsing the solution may reveal that the solution just won't work. If so, another solution should be sought.

Does anything about the solution need to be changed? Rehearsing the solution may reveal that certain aspects of it need modification or 'fine-tuning'.

Does it reveal any doubts, reservations and objections to the solution? Rehearsing the solution sometimes reveals to the coachee that they have a doubt, reservation or objection to some aspect of the solution and its implementation. This can be discussed and worked through with the coach.

Types of solution rehearsal

Here are a variety of ways in which the coachee can rehearse their solution in the session:

Behavioural practice. Behavioural practice allows the coachee to practise a solution that calls for a change in their behaviour (e.g.

role play). It can also help the coachee to gain experience of their cognitive solution (e.g. staying silent while practising tolerance of silence).

Cognitive-behavioural practice. The best way to change an attitude is to think and act in ways that are consistent with the desired attitude. While rehearsing the solution in the session, the coachee holds in mind the desired attitude while engaging in relevant behavioural practice. Chairwork can be helpful here (see Kellogg, 2015).

Mental rehearsal. Mental rehearsal involves the coachee imagining themself implementing the solution in their mind's eye. It is often referred to as imagery work. Here, the coachee can mentally rehearse any of the solutions mentioned earlier. They can do this to prepare themself to implement the solution in everyday life.

Once the client has had an opportunity to practise their chosen solution in the session and has processed and discussed their experience with the therapist, then the coach should help the coachee to develop an action plan.

Developing an action plan and implementing it

In ongoing problem-focused coaching, the coach would encourage the coachee to begin the process of change by negotiating with them a specific homework assignment where the coachee would implement using the agreed solution preferably in the face of adversity while using the concept known as 'challenging not overwhelming' (Dryden, 1985b) – see Chapter 23. In the following session, the coach would review the homework assignment with the coachee, and the process would follow the same principle, i.e. negotiation and review of specific homework assignments at the end and beginning of coaching sessions. Something akin to this process does feature in OAATC where the coach and coachee agree to meet one session at a time. In coaching which lasts for one or two sessions, the focus is on the creation of a general action plan rather than on specific assignments. When helping the coachee devise an action plan, the coach should encourage them to use their strengths and other resources that the coach helped them to identify earlier.

This action plan should ideally involve a commitment to implement the solution as frequently as possible as long as doing so can be implemented into the coachee's life. The plan should be created with achieving the coachee's goal very much in both the coach's and coachee's minds. Possible roadblocks should be identified and dealt with in advance as discussed in the following chapter.

Identifying and dealing with roadblocks[1]

The SSC/OAATC coach has to walk a fine line between encouraging the coachee to be optimistic about achieving their development-based objective (in development-focused SSC/OAATC) or their problem-related goal (in problem-focused SSC/OAATC) and to be realistic in that they may experience a roadblock along this route.

Thus, it is important before ending the session for the coach to encourage the coachee to think about what possible roadblocks they might encounter as they work towards their development-based objective or problem-based goal so that they can give some thought to how they can avoid the roadblock or have a plan to deal with it should they encounter it. This chapter explains how to identify and deal with roadblocks.

Dealing with anticipated roadblocks in development-focused SSC/OAATC

In this section, I will deal with helping the coachee to identify the roadblock separately from encouraging them to develop a plan to deal with it. Both of these tasks have to be done quite quickly given the time constraints of development-focused SSC/OAATC.

Helping the coachee to identify the roadblock

One sign that a coachee might be experiencing a roadblock in their journey towards achieving their development-based objective is that they are not working towards this objective at a time when they might expect themself to do so. In short, they are procrastinating on doing the task. Here are a number of questions that the coach might ask the coachee on this issue to discover reasons for the procrastinating:

- What might you be avoiding at this point?
- What types of things do you typically procrastinate over? Are any of these relevant to the procrastination you would be doing here?
- What would have to be in place for you to resume your work towards your objective?
- If I could give you one thing that would lead you to resume your work towards the objective what would it be?

Helping the coachee to develop a plan to deal with the roadblock

Once the reason for the procrastination has been determined, the coach would then help the coachee develop a plan to deal with the anticipated roadblock so that it does not occur or have a plan to deal with it if it does occur.

A common anticipated obstacle here is when the coach believes that they have to be in the mood to work towards their objective. If the coach can help them see that while this would be nice, it is still possible for them to do the required work without being in the mood and they are prepared to act on this then either they will encounter the obstacle or they will have a good plan in place to deal with it once they notice themself procrastinating due to them not being in the mood to do the work.

When a coachee seeks problem-focused SSC/OAATC for a coaching-related obstacle in their work with another coach, this occurs either because they did not have a plan to deal with a roadblock that could have been foreseen or because something happened that could not have been anticipated, and thus the coachee could not have been expected to have a plan in place to deal with it[2].

Finally, it is important for the coach to remind the coachee of their strengths since one of these variables may be useful in dealing with the anticipated roadblock.

Doing lapse prevention work in problem-focused SSC/OAATC

It is possible to distinguish between a lapse (a brief and minor return to a problem state) and a relapse (a 'back to square one' and more enduring return to a problem state). Relapse tends to occur when a coachee has not dealt adequately with lapses. Consequently, just before the ending process, the coach needs to help the coachee recognise the human tendency to lapse and to respond to a lapse as soon as it happens in order to ward off a relapse occurring. Drawing on the suggestions of Hoyt and Rosenbaum (2018), the coach might ask the coachee a question such as:

- "What would be a sign that this problem was coming back? How can you respond if you notice that this was happening?"

Other questions might involve the coachee again using their nominated strengths and resources. For example:

- "Which of your strengths can you call on if you notice yourself slipping back into your problem?"
- "If you notice that you have lapsed, who might support you in dealing with it?"

Summarising, moving forward and tying-up loose ends

At this point of the process, the coach and coachee are moving towards the end of the session, and it is important that the ending is a good one. In order for this to happen, the coach asks the coachee to summarise their work together, encourages them to engage in a process that I call the 'reflect–digest–take action–let time pass–decision-making' process, tie up any loose ends and make concrete plans for a follow-up.

Summarising

Before ending the session, it is important for the coach to ask the coachee to summarise the session and what they are going to take away with them. Asking the coachee to provide the summary is in keeping with the importance that they are active throughout the process. It also helps the coach to note any omissions and to fill in the blanks where indicated.

Summarising in development-focused SSC/OAATC

A good summary in development-focused SSC/OAATC should contain:

- The coachee's development-based objective and why it is important to them
- Their action plan and how they will implement it
- Their plan to deal with any anticipated roadblocks

Summarising in problem-focused SSC/OAATC

A good summary in problem-focused SSC/OAATC should contain:

- The coachee's problem and goal or just goal (in solution-focused coaching)
- The work done on the problem and/or towards the goal
- What the coachee learned during this work
- The solution the coachee selected and the strengths and resources they can draw on to deal with its implementation and any lapses experienced
- The action plan the coachee developed with the coach to achieve their problem-related goal

Inviting the coachee to reflect on the work, digest it, take action on it and let time pass before making a decision on seeking further coaching

As we have seen SSC/OAATC is a way of working where the coach and coachee work together to help the coachee get the most out of the meeting knowing it may be the only session they may have, but knowing that more coaching may be available. As this will be the coachee's decision, it is very useful if at this point the coach invites the coachee to engage in a five-stage process that I have called the 'reflect–digest–take action–letting time pass–decision-making' process (Dryden, 2019a).

Reflection

When the coachee reflects on the session, they go over it and see what they have learned and what they are going to take forward from it. They may do this reflection privately or discuss it with supportive friends.

Digestion

Digesting what they have learned involves the coachee thinking more deeply about: i) the relevant issue, ii) how they might experiment with other related solutions and iii) how they could apply their chosen solution to other situations if it proves useful.

Taking action

The coachee needs to take action either to implement their development-related action plan or to implement their solution to the problem discussed in the session and, if necessary, to other problems. The coachee might also experiment with other forms of action as relevant that they may have thought about while in the digestion stage.

Letting time pass

After an active period of reflection, digestion and action, the coachee can then be advised to let things settle down and let time pass to see how they feel about whether or not they need more coaching.

Decision

In my view, the value of SSC/OAATC lies in the fact that the coachee knows that they can come back for another session if they need to. Knowing this means that the coachee may not take up this offer, particularly if they are doing well. If not, they can choose to come back at a time convenient to them. Such a decision is enhanced by the coachee engaging in the four stages previously discussed.

Tying up any loose ends

When the session ends, it is essential that the coachee leaves with a sense of completeness and optimism about the process. If they have any questions, then they should be encouraged to ask them. Also, if they have some doubts, reservations or objections (DROs) to any aspect of the process, they should be able to express them so that the coach can respond. For example, the SSC/OAATC coach could ask something like: "If when you get home, you realise that you wished you could have asked me something or told me something, what might that be?" or "Do you have any reservations about the work we did today that you would like to discuss with me before we finish?" If a client leaves with their question answered or their reservation expressed and responded to, then they will go away with a sense that they have been 'heard' by the coach as well as taking away a plan to further their development or tackle their problem.

Plan for follow-up

If the coach and coachee are going to have a follow-up (see Chapter 30), then the last thing that they should do is put a date in their respective diaries when this is going to happen and how it is to happen (e.g. by telephone). In this case, I suggest that that coachee initiates the contact on the agreed date.

Following-up

Follow-up occurs at a date agreed by the coach and coachee at the end of their coaching session (e.g. in three months' time). It occurs assuming that the coachee has not sought further coaching help from the coach in the meantime. Follow-up is important, in my view, in that it provides information on outcome, the coachee's view of the session and if relevant, the coachee's view of the service in which SSC/OAATC took place. It is imperative that when the follow-up meeting occurs – and here I will assume that it occurs over the telephone or by Skype – that the session is scheduled for a time and place where the coachee can talk free from distraction and interruption. The coach needs to have the coachee's full attention. Here are some illustrative questions about what the coachee achieved from the session and about the session itself.

Outcome

In this section, I will deal with the outcome from development-focused SSC/OAATC first and then with the outcome from problem-focused SSC/OAATC.

Outcome from development-focused SSC/OAATC

The coach should begin by reminding the coachee what development-based objective they negotiated. Then, the coach should ask:

- "To what extent have you met your objective?"

  The coach might suggest the use of a five-point scale from 'not at all' to 'fully'. If the coachee has met their objective, the coach should ask:
- "What factors led you to bring about this outcome?"
- "What benefits have you experienced from meeting the objective?"
- "Have others noticed any change in you?"

  If the coachee did not meet their objective, the coach should ask:
- "What stopped you from meeting the objective?"
- "What have the consequences been for you as a result of you not meeting the objective?"
- "Have other areas of your life changed for better or worse?"

Outcome from problem-focused SSC/OAATC

The coach should begin by reminding the coachee what problem (or coaching-related obstacle) they sought help for as well as their goal. Then, the coach should ask:

- "To what extent have you achieved your goal?"

  The coach might again suggest the use of a five-point scale from 'not at all' to 'fully'. If the coachee has achieved their goal, the coach should ask:
- "What factors led you to bring about this outcome?"
- "What benefits have you experienced from achieving your goal?"
- "Have others noticed any change in you?"

  If the coachee did not achieve their goal, the coach should ask:
- "What stopped you from achieving your goal?"
- "What have the consequences been for you as a result of not achieving your goal?"
- "Have other areas of your life changed for better or worse?"

The session

Concerning the session itself, the coach should ask:

- "What do you recall from the coaching session you had?"
- "What was particularly helpful or unhelpful about the session?"
- "How satisfied are you with the coaching that you received?"
- "Did you find the single-session (or one-at-time) way of working sufficient?"
- "If not, would you wish to resume coaching? If so, would you like to see another coach?"

Other questions

- "If you had any recommendations for improvement in the service that you received, what would they be?"
- Is there anything else I have not specifically asked you that you would like me to know?"

This brings us to the end of this book. I hope that you have found it valuable. I would welcome any feedback that you have for me. Please send an email to windy@windydryden.com

Notes

I Introducing Single-Session Coaching and One-At-A-Time Coaching (SSC/OAATC)

1. Thoughout this book I will use the abbreviations 'SSC' and 'OAATC' to refer to 'Single-Session Coaching' and 'One-At-A-Time Coaching' respectively.
2. In this book, I will use the terms 'coach' and 'coachee' rather that 'coach' and 'client'.
3. In this book, I will use the term 'objective' to represent what the coachee wants to achieve from development-focused work and the term 'goal' to represent what they want to achieve from problem-focused work.

3 The foundations of SSC/OAATC

1. Problem-focused coaching is focused on helping a coachee address a mild/moderate emotional problem which may occur in the context of coaching in which case it constitutes an obstacle or is the main reason for seeking help (see Chapter 8).

4 People can be helped in one session of coaching or in one coaching session at a time

1. While for the purposes of clarity, I will discuss these two types of coaching separately in this book, in reality they can overlap.

7 Development-focused SSC/OAATC

1. Later on in this book, I will differentiate between an outcome objective and a process objective (see Chapter 21).
2. It may have both, of course, but the intrinsic type predominates.

3 This may be able to be done if coach and coachee agree that more coaching may be available.

8 Problem-focused SSC/OAATC

1 Coaches are also asked to help coachees with their practical problems (Dryden, 2018c). However, I will not cover this topic in this book.
2 Later on in this book, I will differentiate between an outcome goal and a process goal (see Chapter 21).

12 Good practice in SSC/OAATC

1 For a more detailed discussion of this point see Dryden (2019c).

14 Placing SSC/OAATC in context

1 http://dominiquerendalifecoach.com/single-session-coaching/ – accessed 09/02/19.
2 www.briseeley.com/single-session/1-hour-single-session – accessed 09/02/19.

15 Responding to the first contact

1 See Chapter 14 for examples of how coaches list SSC/OAATC on their websites.

16 Contracting for SSC/OAATC

1 I refer the reader to these sources for an extended discussion of this subject. In this chapter I will focus on contracting for SSC/OAATC.
2 Some coaches prefer a written agreement to be signed by both parties, while for others a written statement by the applicant will suffice.
3 See Dryden (2017b) for a full discussion of these three issues.

17 Structuring the session effectively

1. Oxford Dictionaries (online). Oxford, OXF, GBR: Oxford University Press. 2015 – accessed on 18/02/19.
2. In solution-focused coaching this step is omitted.

18 Preparing for the session: The pre-session telephone conversation

1. Although informally 'walk-in' coaching happens frequently in organisations (e.g. where one colleague briefly consults another and gets briefly 'coached').

19 Beginning the session

1. As I described in Chapter 18, this involves the coach asking the coachee a question such as, "Between now and our face-to face-session, I would like to invite you to notice and note down anything that may indicate that things are changing for the better with respect to the problem (or coaching-related obstacle). Are you willing to do that?"

21 Agreeing on a development-based process objective or problem-based process goal

1. I made the decision to use the term 'objective' in development-focused coaching and the term 'goal' in problem-focused coaching to make it clear to which type of coaching I am discussing at any given point.
2. Here the person's coach does not know how to address the problem or has addressed it unsuccessfully. Given this, the coachee is referred to a different coach whose agreed task is to address the coaching-related obstacle.
3. These are known as solution-focused coaches.

23 Facilitating change in SSC/OAATC: General factors

1 When I mention 'problem' here, this includes a coaching-related obstacle.
2 This may not apply to coaches who are solution-focused rather than problem- and solution-focused.
3 Again, this may not apply to coaches who are solution-focused rather than problem- and solution-focused.
4 The concept of 'acceptance' is complex and a full discussion of it is beyond the scope of this book. For those interested, I recommend Chapter 6 in Dryden (2018d).

25 Facilitating change in problem-focused SSC/OAATC

1 See Chapter 21.

28 Identifying and dealing with roadblocks[1]

1 I have previously said that problem-focused SSC/OAATC deals with a coachee's problem or coaching-related obstacle. Since I use the word 'obstacle' in this latter phrase, I refer in this to chapter to the word 'roadblock' to describe anticipated obstacles in *both* development-focused SSC/OAATC *and* problem-focused SSC/OAATC.
2 In this situation the person's coach did not have the skills to help them deal with the unanticipated obstacle and thus referred the person to a coach who could help them with this.

References

Bennett, J.L. (2008). Contracting for success. *International Journal of Coaching in Organizations*, *6*(4), 7–14.

Bloom, B.L. (1981). Focused single-session therapy: Initial development and evaluation. In S. Budman (Ed.), *Forms of Brief Therapy* (pp. 167–216). New York: Guilford Press.

Bloom, B.L. (1992). *Planned Short-Term Psychotherapy: A Clinical Handbook*. Boston, MA: Allyn and Bacon.

Bordin, E.S. (1979). The generalizability of the psychoanalytic concept of the working alliance. *Psychotherapy: Theory, Research and Practice*, *16*, 252–260.

Cavanagh, M.J. (2005). Mental-health issues and challenging clients in executive coaching. In M.J. Cavanagh, A.M. Grant & T. Kemp (Eds.), *Evidence-Based Coaching: Theory, Research and Practice from the Behavioural Sciences*, (pp. 21–36). Bowen Hills, QLD: Australian Academic Press.

de Shazer, S (1985). *Keys to Solution in Brief Therapy*. New York: W.W. Norton.

Dryden, W. (1985a). Cognition without ignition. *Contemporary Psychology*, *30*(10), 788–789.

Dryden, W. (1985b). Challenging but not overwhelming: A compromise in negotiating homework assignments. *British Journal of Cognitive Psychotherapy*, *3*(1), 77–80.

Dryden, W. (2011). *Counselling in a Nutshell*. 2nd Edition. London: Sage.

Dryden, W. (2015). Rational Emotive Behaviour Therapy: Distinctive Features. 2nd edition. Hove, East Sussex: Routledge.

Dryden, W. (2016). *When Time is at a Premium: Cognitive-Behavioural Approaches to Single-Session Therapy and Very Brief Coaching*. London: Rationality Publications.

Dryden, W. (2017a). *Very Brief Cognitive-Behavioural Coaching (VBCBC)*. Abingdon, Oxon: Routledge.

Dryden, W. (2017b). *The Coaching Alliance: Theory and Guidelines for Practice*. Abingdon, Oxon: Routledge.

Dryden, W. (2018a). *Rational Emotive Behavioural Coaching: Distinctive Features*. Abingdon, Oxon: Routledge.

Dryden, W. (2018b). *Very Brief Therapeutic Conversations*. Abingdon, Oxon: Routledge.

Dryden, W. (2018c). *Cognitive-Emotive-Behavioural Coaching: A Flexible and Pluralistic Approach*. Abingdon, Oxon: Routledge.

Dryden, W. (2018d). *The Relevance of Rational Emotive Behaviour Therapy for Modern CBT and Psychotherapy*. Abingdon, Oxon: Routledge.

Dryden, W. (2019a). *Single-Session 'One-At-A-time' Therapy: A Rational Emotive Behaviour Therapy Approach*. Abingdon, Oxon: Routledge.

Dryden, W. (2019b). *Rational Behaviour Therapy in India: Very Brief Therapy for Problems of Daily Living*. Abingdon, Oxon: Routledge.

Dryden, W. (2019c). *Single-Session Therapy: 100 Key Points and Techniques*. Abingdon, Oxon: Routledge.

Dryden, W. (2019d). *Single-Session Therapy: Distinctive Features*. Abingdon, Oxon: Routledge.

Eccles, J.S., & Wigfield, A. (2002). Motivational beliefs, values and goals. *Annual Review of Psychology*, 53, 109–132.

Fielder, J.H., & Starr, L.M. (2008). What's the big deal about coaching contracts. *International Journal of Coaching in Organizations*, 6(4), 15–27.

Freud, S., & Breuer, J. (1895). *Studien Über Hysterie*. Leipzig and Vienna: Deuticke.

Garvin, C.D., & Seabury, B.A. (1997). *Interpersonal Practice in Social Work: Promoting Competence and Social Justice*. 2nd Edition. Boston, MA: Allyn & Bacon.

Hill, J., & Oliver, J. (2019). *Acceptance and Commitment Coaching: Distinctive Features*. Abingdon, Oxon: Routledge.

Hoyt, M.F. (2000). *Some Stories are Better than Others: Doing What Works in Brief Therapy and Managed Care*. Philadelphia, PA: Brunner/Mazel.

Hoyt, M.F. (2011). Foreword. In A. Slive & M. Bobele (Eds.), *When One Hour is All You Have: Effective Therapy for Walk-in Clients* (pp. xix–xv). Phoenix, AZ: Zeig, Tucker, & Theisen.

REFERENCES

Hoyt, M.F. (2018). Single-session therapy: Stories, structures, themes, cautions, and prospects. In M.F. Hoyt, M. Bobele, A. Slive, J. Young, J., & M. Talmon (Eds.), *Single-Session Therapy by Walk-In or Appointment: Administrative, Clinical, and Supervisory Aspects of One-at-a-Time Services* (pp. 155–174). New York: Routledge.

Hoyt, M.F., Bobele, M., Slive, A., Young, J., & Talmon, M. (Eds.) (2018). *Single-Session Therapy by Walk-In or Appointment: Administrative, Clinical, and Supervisory Aspects of One-at-a Time Services*. New York: Routledge.

Hoyt, M.F., & Rosenbaum, R. (2018). Some ways to end an SST. In M.F. Hoyt, M. Bobele, A. Slive, J. Young, J., & M. Talmon (Eds.), *Single-Session Therapy by Walk-In or Appointment: Administrative, Clinical, and Supervisory Aspects of One-at-a Time Services* (pp. 318–323). New York: Routledge.

Hoyt, M.F., & Talmon, M.F. (Eds.). (2014). *Capturing the Moment: Single Session Therapy and Walk-In Services*. Bethel, CT: Crown House Publishing.

Hoyt, M.F., Talmon, M., & Rosenbaum, R. (1990). Sixty attempts for planned single-session therapy. Unpublished paper.

Keller, G., & Papasan, J. (2012). *The One Thing: The Surprisingly Simple Truth Behind Extraordinary Results*. Austin, TX: Bard Press.

Kellogg, S. (2015). *Transformational Chairwork: Using Psychotherapeutic Dialogues in Clinical Practice*. Lanham, MD: Rowman & Littlefield.

Kuehn, J.L. (1965). Encounter at Leyden: Gustav Mahler consults Sigmund Freud. *Psychoanalytic Review*, *52*, 345–364.

Lane, D.A., & Corrie, S. (2009). Does coaching psychology need the concept of formulation? *International Coaching Psychology Review*, *4(2), 193–206.*

Lee, R.J. (2013). The role of contracting in coaching: Balancing individual client and organizational issues. In J. Passmore, D.B. Peterson, & T. Freire (Eds.), *The Psychology of Coaching and Mentoring* (pp. 40–57). Chichester, West Sussex: John Wiley & Sons.

Lonergan. J. (2012, Autumn). 'I alone must do it, but I cannot do it alone'. Inside Out, Issue 68. [http://iahip.org/inside-out/issue-68-autumn-2012/i-alone-must-do-it-but-i-cannot-do-it-alone-a-talk-by-john-lonergan-a-decade-on-10th-anniversary-celebration-of-inside-out] (accessed 16 February 2019).

Neenan, M. (2018). *Cognitive-Behavioural Coaching: Distinctive Features*. Abingdon, Oxon: Routledge.

Simon, G.E., Imel, Z.E., Ludman, E.J., & Steinfeld, B.J. (2012). Is dropout after a first psychotherapy visit always a bad outcome? *Psychiatric Services*, *63*(7), 705–707.

Slive, A., & Bobele, M. (Eds) (2011). *When One Hour is All You Have: Effective Therapy for Walk-in Clients*. Phoenix, AZ: Zeig, Tucker & Theisen.

Slive, A., & Bobele, M. (2014). Walk-in single session therapy: Accessible mental health services. In M.F. Hoyt & M. Talmon (Eds.), *Capturing the Moment: Single Session Therapy and Walk-in Services* (pp. 73–94). Bethel, CT: Crown House Publishing.

Slive, A., & Bobele, M. (2018). The three top reasons why walk-in/single sessions make perfect sense. In M.F. Hoyt, M. Bobele, A. Slive, J. Young, J., & M. Talmon (Eds.), *Single-Session Therapy by Walk-In or Appointment: Administrative, Clinical, and Supervisory Aspects of One-at-a Time Services* (pp. 27–39). New York: Routledge.

Talmon, M. (1990). *Single Session Therapy: Maximising the Effect of the First (and Often Only) Therapeutic Encounter*. San Francisco, CA: Jossey-Bass.

Talmon, M. (1993). *Single Session Solutions: A Guide to Practical, Effective and Affordable Therapy*. New York: Addison-Wesley.

Utry, Z. A., Palmer, S., McLeod, J., & Cooper, M. (2019). Pluralistic Coaching. In S. Palmer & A. Whybrow (Eds.), *Handbook of Coaching Psychology: A Guide for Practitioners* (pp. 134–166). 2nd Edition. Abingdon, Oxon: Routledge.

Whitmore, J. (2017). *Coaching for Performance: The Principles and Practice of Coaching and Leadership*. 5th Edition. London: Nicholas Brearley Publishing.

Young, J. (2018). SST: The misunderstood gift that keeps on giving. In M.F. Hoyt, M. Bobele, A. Slive, J. Young, & M. Talmon (Eds.), *Single-Session Therapy by Walk-In or Appointment: Administrative, Clinical, and Supervisory Aspects of One-at-a-Time Services* (pp. 40–58). New York: Routledge.

Index

acceptance 107, 146
'Acceptance and Commitment Coaching' (Hill & Oliver) 100
action 109–111, 124, 137
action plans 15, 19, 84, 135; developing/devising 123–124, 128–129; development-focused coaching 32, 36; development-focused SSC/OAATC 30–31, 72, 75, 109; implementing 31, 124, 128–129; integrating into life 124; obstacles 30; problem-focused coaching 15, 128; problem-focused SSC/OAATC 35–36, 75; timeline 123
additional sessions 46–47
adversity 118–122; changing 122; healthy attitude towards 119–121; questioning 121–122; reframing 121
alliance-building 72
applicants: contracting 69–70; role 64, 65, 66
appointments 71
assessed problems 96–97
assessment 58

behaviour change 116
behavioural goals 97–98
behavioural practice 127–128
behavioural solutions 126
being helped by others 101–103
Bloom, Bernard 5, 5–6
bonds 37
Bordin, Ed 37
brief encounters 11
budget holders 46

capsule summaries 56
case conceptualisation 58
chairwork 128
challenging not overwhelming 109–110, 118, 128
change: coachees readiness for 78; facilitating 30, 105, 113–116; general factors 105–111; noticing 84, 86
clarity 58
coachees: coaching, not therapy 5; doubts, reservations or objections (DROs) 54, 127, 138; engagement of 52; experience problems in coaching

151

4–5; information provided by 69–70, 83; readiness to change 78; readiness for work 13; resources 14, 54; role of 64; understanding 54; volunteering to be coached 25
coaches: benefits of SSC/OAATC for 42–43; good, criteria for 41–42; liberal use of questions 54; prudently active 52; training workshops 25
coaching: long-term 48; previous 54; skills 47, 48; traditional approach 17
coaching contracts 67–69; expandable length of 12; length of, influential 12–13
coaching, not therapy 5
coaching-related obstacles 95–97, 132–133, 146
'coaching speeded up' 47
cognitive-behavioural practice 128
cognitive-behavioural solutions 126
commitment 129
consent 67, 70
context of SSC/OAATC 59–61
contracting 67–70, 69–70, 144
Cooper, M. 52
core values 80, 82, 100, 111
cost 26
counselling services 25

de Shazer, Steve 83, 86
dead time 71
decision 137
delivery, mode of 22, 45
development 4
development-based objective 8, 9, 14, 17, 18, 19, 30, 34, 38, 42, 69, 80, 99, 103, 105, 131, 132, 135; agreeing on 94–95; facilitating change 113–116; monitoring progress 123

development-focused coaching 143, 145; action plans 32, 36; assessment 58; change, facilitating 105, 116; emphasis 13, 29, 90; focus 14, 15, 18, 53; good practice elements 57, 58; objectives 93; obstacles to progress 29, 33, 78; one-at-a-time 32; positive reasons for offering 23–24; possible achievements 18–19; roadblocks 109, 110; single-session 32, 36; SSC/OAATC replaces 45; take aways 55; terminology 145

development-focused SSC/OAATC: action 109; action plans 30–31, 72, 75, 109; as appropriate 66; assessment 58; benefits for coaches 42; change factors 105, 113–116; change of behaviour 116; conditions to facilitate 30; emphasis 13, 29, 78; expectation 105–106; features of 30; focus 89–90; good practice elements 53, 55; objectives 53, 72, 93, 93–95, 145; outcome 139–140; pre-session telephone contact 79–81; possible achievements 18–19; realism 106; roadblocks 109, 110, 131–132; session structuring 14–15; summarising 135; working alliance in 37–39

digestion 137
discomfort tolerance 107–108
dissatisfaction 4
disturbance 4
domain, identifying 18
doubts, reservations or objections (DROs) 54, 127, 138
drop-outs 6

emotional impact 54–55
emotive goals 97–98

INDEX

enquirer role 64, 65
environment 115–116
environmental solutions 126
expectations 13, 52, 66, 105–106
explicitness 58
explorer role 63–64
external resources 82, 102–103, 124, 129
external support 54, 80, 82, 103, 133

first contact 65–66
focus 52–53, 57, 89–92; development-focused coaching 14, 15, 18, 53; development-focused SSC/OAATC 89–90; maintaining 33–34, 91–92; off 92; problem-focused SSC/OAATC 33–34, 90
follow-up sessions 138, 140–141
following though 75
Freud, Sigmund 5
further sessions 6, 8–9, 19, 32, 46–47, 48, 56, 61, 68, 85, 87, 95, 136, 139
future orientation 53

Garvin, C.D. 64
geography 26
goals 13, 15, 34–35, 38, 53, 65, 95–98, 143; problem-based 14, 19, 38, 42, 69, 80, 93, 97, 131
good practice 52–56
GROW model 7, 24
guiding principles 80–81, 82, 102

help-seeking roles 63–64, 65
helping others 100–101
helping preferences 81, 82–83
Hill, J. 100
histories, taking 57
homework assignments 60, 128

honesty 100, 102, 111
Hoyt, Michael 5, 6, 9, 74, 133

inference 26, 119, 121–122, 126
informed consent 67, 70
intentionality 12–13
internal strengths 14, 53, 79, 82, 84, 99, 124, 129
interruptions 91–92

Kaiser Permanente Clinic, San Francisco 5
Keller, G. 55
Kellogg, S. 128

lapse prevention work 133
learning preferences 83
learning styles 54, 83
letting time pass 137
listening 57
Lonergan. J. 80
loose ends 56, 137–138

McLeod, J. 52
meaningful points 55
mental rehearsal 128
mindset 21–22, 45, 48, 113–115
misconceptions about SSC/OAATC 45–48
mood 132

objectives 29–30, 53, 72, 93–95, 143, 145
obstacles 19, 30, 31, 36, 65, 72, 95, 145; coaching-related 95–97, 132–133, 146; to progress 29, 33, 78; *see also* roadblocks
Oliver, J. 100
One-At-A-Time Coaching (OAATC) 68–69
One-At-A-Time Therapy 5–6, 9, 20, 25–26

153

outcome: development-focused SSC/OAATC 139–140; problem-focused SSC/OAATC 140
outcome goals 98
outcome objectives 93–95, 143

pacing 58
Palmer, S. 52
Papasan, J. 55
perspective 84
pluralistic foundations of SSC/OAATC 51–52
practice elements to avoid in SSC/OAATC 57–58
pre-session forms *73–74*
pre-session telephone contact 67, 71–72, 77, 99; absence of 87; general questions 78–79; other questions 83; questions relevant to development-focused SSC/OAATC 79–81; questions relevant to problem-focused SSC/OAATC 81–83; sessions linked to 86–87; sufficient 84
problem-based goals 14, 19, 38, 42, 69, 80, 93, 97, 131
problem-focused coaching: action planning 15, 128; challenging not overwhelming 109–110; change, facilitating 105; defined 143; emphasis 29, 33, 117; focus 143; goals 13, 15, 98; good practice elements 57, 58; homework assignments 128; one-at-a-time 33, 95; outcome goals 98; possible achievements 19–20; process goals 98; roadblocks 110; single-session 24, 33, 95; SSC/OAATC replaces 45; take aways 55; terminology 145
problem-focused SSC/OAATC: action 109–110; action plans 35–36, 75; addressing problems, finding solutions 35; adversity and 118–122; agreeing solutions 125–126; as appropriate 66; behavioural goals 97–98; benefits for coaches 42; change factors 105, 117–122; change noticed 86; criteria 33; discomfort tolerance 107–108; emotive goals 97–98; emphasis 78; goals 53; goals in 95–98; good practice elements 52; keeping focus 33–34, 90; lapse prevention work 133; obstacles 36; outcome 140; outcome goals 98; positive reasons for offering 24; pre-session telephone contact 81–83; process goals 98; realism 106–107; rehearsing solution in-session 127–128; roadblocks 132–133; roadblocks in 110; role models 102; session structuring 72; setting problem-related goals 34–35; summarising 136; terminology 146; types of solutions 126; understanding target problem 34
problems: assessed 96–97; factors that maintain 117–118; previous attempts to solve 100; stated 96; successful attempts 100
procedure, explaining 53
process goals 98
process objectives 93, 94–95, 143

questionnaire 77
quick fixes 46

rapport 57–58
Rational Emotive Behavioural Coaching (REBC) 7, 24
realism 106–107
referrals 146

INDEX

reflect-digest-take action-let time pass process 9, 68
reflection 136
reframing 121
relapse 133
research 35–36
resiliency 14, 53, 79, 82, 84, 99
roadblocks 108, 109, 110, 129, 131–133, 135, 146; *see also* obstacles
role models 84, 102
Rosenbaum, Richard 5, 6, 133

sample coaching 24–25
scepticism 36
Seabury, B.A. 64
sessions: beginning 85–87; coaching variables 99–103; further 56, 68, 75; linked to pre-session contact 86–87; phase 1: the pre-session phase 71–72, *73–74*; phase 2: the early phase 72; phase 3: the middle phase 72, 75; phase 4: the late phase 75; phase 5: the follow-through phase 75; purpose of 85–86; structuring 71–75; summaries 55–56; what can be achieved 18–20
side-effects 125–126
signposts 19
Simon, G.E. et al 36
Single-Session Coaching and One-At-A-Time Coaching (SSC/OAATC): misconceptions about 45–48; nature of 85–86, 87; positive reasons for offering 23–24; positive reasons for seeking 24–25; pragmatic reasons for offering 25–26; pragmatic reasons for seeking 26–27; vs traditional coaching 17–18; value of 137

Single-Session Coaching (SSC): description 7–8, 19; indistinguishable from OAATC 20; more is available 8–9; nature of 7–9; scenario 1 7l; scenario 2 7; scenario 3 7–8; scenario 4 8
Single-Session Therapy (SST) 5–6, 8, 46
skeleton key technique 83, 145
solution-focused coaches 95, 145, 146
solution-focused SSC/OAATC 125
solution rehearsal 127–128
SSC/OAATC *see* Single-Session Coaching and One-At-A-Time Coaching (SSC/OAATC)
stated problems 96
summarising 55–56, 135, 136

take aways 55
taking action 137
Talmon, Moshe 5–6
tasks 35
team, concept of 80
telephone conversations *see* pre-session telephone contact
time 27, 48
timelines 123

Utry, Z. A. 52

value-based action 110–111
values 80, 82, 99–100
views 37–38

waiting lists 25–26
walk-in therapy 77, 145
websites, coaches' 59–61, 64–66
working alliance in SSC/OAATC 37–39

Young, J. 21, 61